Jan 20

AF182200

Jeremy,

Looking forward to seeing you next week. Happy reading,

with best wishes

Charlie

THE JAPAN HEALTHCARE DEBATE

DIVERSE PERSPECTIVES

ABOUT THE AUTHOR

Mark A. Colby first came to Japan in 1978. He has a bachelor's degree in biology and attended The University of Washington's School of Dentistry. He began his career with Abbott Laboratories and worked for them both in the US and Japan. Since leaving Abbott, Colby has established five businesses in Japan, all focused on the evolving Japan healthcare scene. Colby is the author of dozens of reports and publications about healthcare in Japan including the well-received *Negotiating the Gray Maze, the Business of Medicine in Japan* (co-author). He has chaired many American Chamber of Commerce in Japan healthcare-related committees including, Diagnostics, Medical Devices, and Medical Services. He currently serves as the chairperson of the ACCJ Healthcare Committee.

THE JAPAN HEALTHCARE DEBATE

DIVERSE PERSPECTIVES

Mark A. Colby

EDITED BY STEVE ZIOLKOWSKI

GLOBAL
ORIENTAL

THE JAPAN HEALTHCARE DEBATE
DIVERSE PERSPECTIVES

by Mark A. Colby

First published 2004 by

GLOBAL ORIENTAL
PO Box 219
Folkestone
Kent CT20 3WP
UK

www.globaloriental.co.uk

British Library Cataloguing in Publication Data
A CIP catalogue entry for this book is available from the British Library

ISBN 1-901903-33-8

Set in Gill Sans 10.5 on 12pt by Mark Heslington, Scarborough, North Yorkshire
Printed and bound in England by Cromwell Press, Trowbridge, Wilts

Contents

This book is dedicated to
my two daughters, Julie and Yoko

List of Figures

Acknowledgements

This book would not have been possible without the valuable contributions of a great many people. I want to especially thank the following people who have made a special effort to contribute to and review this manuscript during its creation.

(In alphabetical order)

Mark Gresham – President, United Publishers Services
William Hall – President, Isis Research, Japan
Guy Harris, D.O. – President, Digital Medical Communications Corp. and Chair of the ACCJ Healthcare Services Committee
Doug Jackson – Communications Director, American Chamber of Commerce in Japan
Takahiko Kaneko – Publishing Director, Edition Synapse
Tadashi Kawai, M.D., Ph.D. – A towering force in clinical laboratory medicine and the primary architect of Japan's laboratory accreditation programs
Koichi Kawabuchi, M.B.A. – Healthcare Economist
Saburo Kimura – Advisor to Johnson & Johnson, Japan and former US Embassy Commercial Officer
P. Reed Maurer, M.Sc. – President, Nippon Pharma Promotions
Paul Norbury – Managing Director, Global Oriental Ltd
John Rogers M.D. – Medical Director, Allergan Japan
Fumimaro Takaku, M.D., Ph.D. – President, Jichi Medical School
Huimin Wang, M.D., M.B.A. – President, Edwards Lifescience K.K and Chair of the ACCJ Medical Device, Imaging and Diagnostics Subcommittee

Donald Westmore – Executive Director, American Chamber of Commerce in Japan
John Wocher, M.H.A. – Vice President, Kamada Medical Center
Steve Ziolkowski – Former Managing Director of Oxford University Japan, now working as a freelance writer, editor, and translator

Foreword

Is Japan's healthcare system a functional giant with a few minor aches and pains or an aging, broken-down hulk? As the title of Mark Colby's book implies, no consensus has formed on the state of healthcare in Japan. Heated debate rages over even what the problems are, let alone how they should be solved.

Calling on his more than twenty-five years in Japan as an entrepreneur in the healthcare industry, Mark Colby has consulted with a broad selection of Japan's healthcare industry leaders and done extensive research on what is needed to put the country's complex healthcare system into perspective and the options available to it. The result is a personalized and seasoned view of Japan's healthcare system in which Mr Colby examines the system's financial health, related medicine, and the medical profession itself. He has gathered views from all along the spectrum of opinion – from supporters of the current system to those who advocate radical surgery – and paired them into two opposed but easily understandable viewpoints that include alternative policy prescriptions.

The American Chamber of Commerce in Japan does not specifically endorse the views in Mr Colby's book, but welcomes its publication as an effort to move the discussion forward. We believe *The Japan Healthcare Debate* will serve as a catalyst in clarifying the issues and developing effective policies to protect and improve the health of all people living and working in Japan.

AMERICAN CHAMBER OF COMMERCE IN JAPAN

Preface

Last year (2003) I was in a meeting that included an official from the Japan Medical Association (JMA). He listened sleepily to me as well as to some other so-called healthcare experts who babbled on about what we saw as the inadequacies of the Japanese healthcare system. When we ran out of things to say, he drew heavily on his cigarette and blew the smoke in our direction. He said, 'You Americans. You're always on a diet. Everyone sweats their guts out in the gym. You can't even find a place to smoke. And do you know what I see?' He paused for effect. 'I see cows walking all over the place disguised as people. I see huge sections of your population in terrible health. Hell, I don't even know why we're even here talking about this stuff. We Japanese live a good ten years longer than you do and we spend less money doing so!' He shook his head, walked to the door grunting under his breath, and left. Hard as it was to swallow, in fact he was right. The truth is that there *is* a lot right about healthcare in Japan. Demographic data plainly suggests that in virtually all categories, the Japanese are the healthiest people on earth. The United States, on the other hand, is somewhere in the middle of the pack at best.

To be more specific about the positive aspects of Japanese healthcare, let us unequivocally state that Japan has the world's best infant mortality rates as well as the longest life-spans for both males and females. Japan also provides access to universal healthcare – a right enshrined in the country's constitution. Given these facts, in all outward respects, Japan does have the best healthcare system in the world, and the World Health Organization endorses this highly flattering evaluation.

Figure 1. Infant deaths per thousand births (1999)

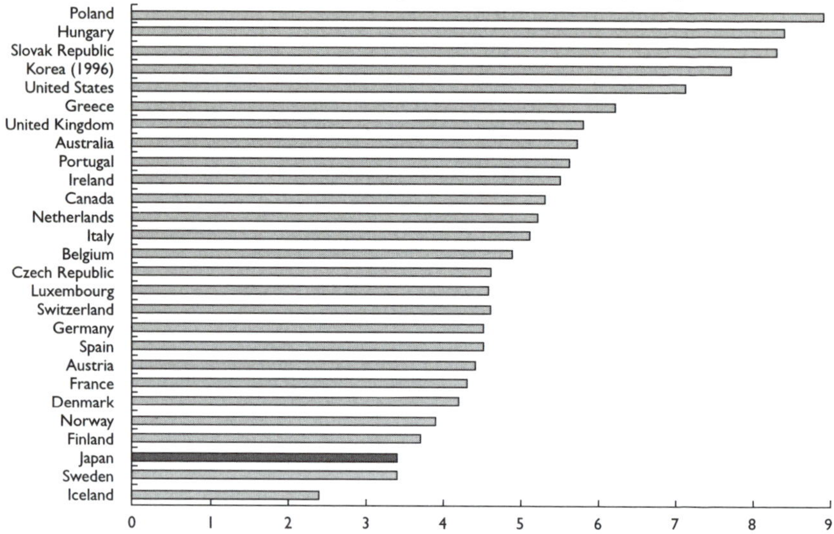

Source: OECD Health Data. 1996 is the latest data available for Korea.

So, what is the problem? In the opinion of this author and many of the contributors to this book, there is a lot wrong. Many of these problems are ones, we believe, that can be solved by common sense. Other issues are matters of scientific debate. Some can be attributed to cultural norms and differences. At this early point in our discussion, however, we will avoid most of these debatable issues because they are dealt with later. But there is one issue that is so clear and so obvious that it cannot be debated or refuted. The plain and simple fact is that maintaining Japan's current healthcare system could well bankrupt the second largest economy in the world.

The Ministry of Health, Labour and Welfare (MHLW) has published statistics indicating that from 2020 maintaining the current system will cost $800 billion per year and will remain at that level for some fifteen years. To put it another way, this is a $12,000 billion problem that will not go away. Looking at it from yet one more perspective, the cost of treating Japanese patients from the year 2020 to 2035 could well equal 25% of Japan's total projected GDP for that period.

A question often asked in relation to Japan's future healthcare costs is whether or not this is a problem for the United States and other industrialized countries? Recently the American Chamber of Commerce in Japan (ACCJ) has been vocal about some of the problems it sees in Japanese healthcare and has put forward views on the subject. Countering the American perspective, the Japan Medical Association (JMA) and other groups have lashed back in the most virulent terms. 'This is none of your business,' is their response. 'This is a domestic issue and the US should stay out of it,' they say. On the surface, these critics of the American criticism have a point. American policy-makers would most certainly not welcome Japan meddling in the US healthcare system and offering unwanted advice. But in the opinion of this author and some contributors to this volume, it is America's business for the following reasons:

1. If the Japanese government ignores the problem, the effects could not only be devastating to Japan, but to the entire world economy – including that of the US. The US needs to be concerned with this problem in much the same way it needs to be interested in the current banking crisis. With the global, interlinked nature of the world economy, if one major player sneezes, the others catch a cold.
2. Solving some of Japan's healthcare problems could mean big business for many American companies. Whether high technology devices, innovative pharmaceutical products, computing solutions, or even new insurance products, the United States is a world leader in nearly all the areas that could help improve the Japanese healthcare situation.

METHODOLOGY

Setting out on this project, my idea was to contact some of the most widely recognized industry leaders in Japanese healthcare. Together with these experts I wanted to go through the process of identifying the system's problems and then try and define some concrete solutions – with special attention as to how US goods and services might contribute to these solutions.

To meet these rather ambitious objectives, I drew upon my network of business people, medical professionals, and government officials. Because all these individuals have spent most of their lives selling to, working in, or regulating the Japanese healthcare system, I felt quite strongly that there would be areas of general consensus and issues on which we all would agree. Well, I was wrong. Was I ever wrong. Instead, what I found was both fascinating and startling. Where

I thought there would be consensus there was disagreement. Where I expected agreement there were any number of diverse views. When it comes to Japanese healthcare, I found, there is in fact very little consensus or agreement at all – even at the most basic level of defining what the problems are, let alone the solutions.

At first, I felt a bit overwhelmed by the task ahead. But sitting in a hot bath one evening, the answer came to me. I remembered a book I had read years ago that focused on the different perspectives of the Germans, French, Americans, and English during World War II entitled *The Anatomy of Peace,* by Emery Reves. The book begins with this paraphrased quote: 'NOTHING can distort the true picture of conditions and events in this world more than to regard one's own perspective [meaning, country] as the center of the universe, and to view things solely in their relationship to that fixed point.' I recall being struck at the time by how incredibly different were the views on the war depending on national and individual perspective. Even as to what constituted good and evil, the honest perspectives of informed and intelligent people varied widely. In other words, perspective is everything.

While the parallel I am drawing is not an exact one, the issues, problems, and possible solutions confronting the Japanese healthcare system are ones that can and must be defined by the varied perspectives of individual experts. To make things even more complicated, I fear that many of these perspectives are hard-wired into the psyche of society and the individuals who comprise it. Thus, my challenge took another turn, although an arguably less ambitious one. Previously, I had been trying to define the problems and offer some solutions. My new goal was to simply try and understand and compare the differing perspectives that a variety of experts have on the very vexing and complex issues that constitute Japanese healthcare.

Common sense dictates that, when it comes to their views about the Japanese healthcare system, physicians would have one united perspective, medical business leaders a different one, and government regulators yet another. In fact, although this grouping, if you will, is generally the case, the polarities are not as clear as I expected. Even within each respective group, opinions and emotions vary greatly. As a result, whenever outlining a certain perspective on a certain issue, I have not categorized the viewpoints as the 'physician's' or the 'bureaucrat's' perspective because it is not as cleanly divided along party lines as one might think. In some cases, you will be able to guess pretty accurately as to which group leans in which direction, but you would probably be surprised to learn the wide range of viewpoints even within particular peer groups.

You will note that I have attempted to delineate issues into only two different perspectives. In many cases, this is admittedly a poorly fabricated and artificial device but I have done so simply to give order to this book and make it more coherent and easier to access. Most of the issues that are examined are extremely complicated. Most of them also have so many conflicting perspectives emanating from groups and individuals that to list them all would be to confuse rather than clarify. And, since clarification is my goal, I hope you will forgive me some of my simplifications.

Within the various perspectives much of the data that rightly should be footnoted may not be. In many cases, people's perceptions, opinions, and beliefs are simply not verifiable. People do not always back up their comments with hard data but more usually with statements along the lines of, 'I read it in *The New England Journal* . . .' or 'I have been practicing medicine for thirty years and I know . . .' I have chosen to incorporate these kinds of statements – whether or not some assertions are supportable – because people's actual beliefs in themselves are perhaps often the most powerful and irrefutable arguments.

1 Defining the Problem

I. THE PROBLEM OF DEMOGRAPHICS

There is no question about what is happening to the demographics of Japan. By the year 2020, one-quarter of the population will be over 65 years old.

Although these numbers speak of longer lives, they also have other huge implications. Perhaps the one statistic that is the most telling is the one so universal that it remains unchanged throughout the world regardless of country or culture: from the age of 65 to death, individuals will on average spend 80% of their lifetime allotment of healthcare expenses. To make things possibly even worse, this lopsided age-to-expense ratio may be even more problematic in an age where people are living into their nineties and even hundreds with increasing frequency.

Figure 2. International comparison of future aged population ratios
(Age 65 and above)

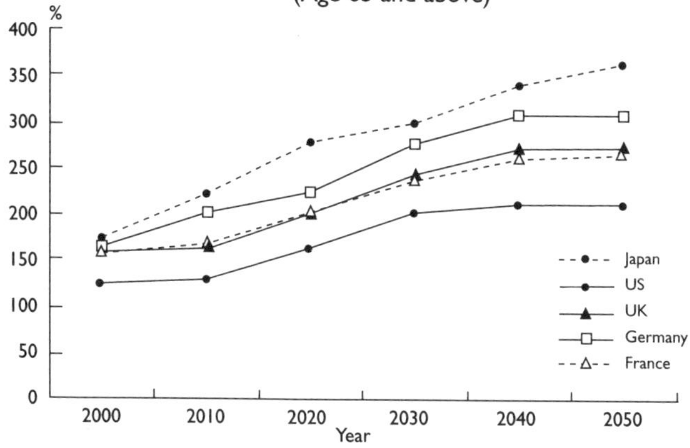

Source: Compiled from United Nations, 'World Population Prospects, 2000 Revision'

PERSPECTIVE A:

AN ELDERLY SOCIETY HAS MANY ADVANTAGES

As Japan grows, so does the collective wisdom of the society: the ability to nurture the next generation or, say, the ability to make good decisions about leadership and continuity. In other words, the ability to work and provide value depends largely on judgment that only age and experience and wisdom can bring. Society needs to do its utmost to engage the older generation and make them useful. Given their large numbers and increasingly advanced age, this generation will have the widest range of lifetime experiences in the history of the world. We need to immediately find ways to harvest this bounty. The elderly need to be used as teachers and mentors for confused youth and directionless young adults. They need to be made useful in corporate boardrooms and to help with complex business decision-making. They should be used as advisors to politicians and bureaucrats. The worst thing we could do is ignore this priceless resourse that is right at our fingertips. These people want to work. These people want to be useful. Through thoughtful legislation we can transform the golden years of our population into a golden future for the generations to come.

PERSPECTIVE B:

JAPANESE POPULATION DEMOGRAPHICS WILL CAUSE MAJOR STRUCTURAL PROBLEMS

As Japan ages, the workforce will shift from a younger, cheaper workforce to an older, less productive and more expensive one. This transformation will decrease Japan's overall competitiveness in terms of both industrial and innovative output. This competitiveness has already forced Japan's most traditional companies to abandon the ideal of lifelong employment, forcing many older employees into unemployment lines. With increasing unemployment adding to the growing number of retirees, tax revenues will drop. If the government chooses to increase taxes, the result will be further decreases in output. If taxes are not increased, social programs will have to be cut back at a time when the demands on the healthcare system and other social programs are skyrocketing.

(Source) 'Public Health of Japan 2002', Japan Public Health Association

The biggest issue surrounding aging demographics is the fact that it is not a short-term problem. It is a gradual process that will last nearly forty years, peaking sometime around the year 2025. No economy in the history of the world has ever faced a challenge of this type or scale. There is no positive way to look at the current demographic trends in modern Japan.

Figure 3. Japan's declining birth and fertility rates

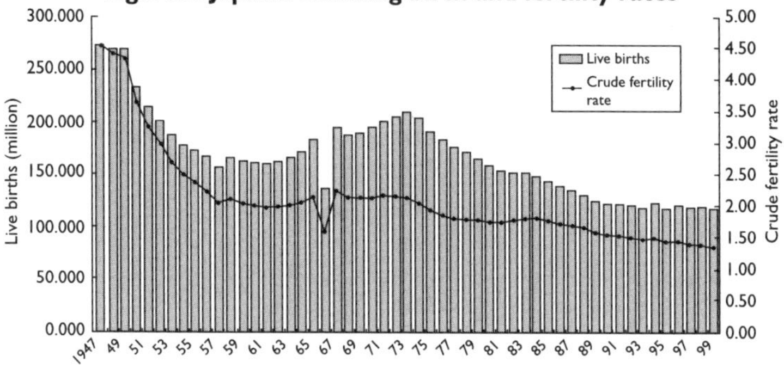

Source: 'Public Health of Japan 2002', Japan Public Health Association

2. THE FINANCIAL HEALTH OF THE SYSTEM

Officially, Japan spends about $300 billion on healthcare yearly, or about 8% of its gross domestic product (GDP). It is noteworthy, however, that these figures do not include over-the-counter pharmaceuticals, health checks, pre-natal care, or any service that is delivered outside the official reimbursement system. Nor does it include the increasing number of supplementary healthcare insurance policies being sold annually. Although no official statistics exist, it is believed that the actual amount spent on healthcare is closer to 12% of Japan's GDP. By comparison, the United States spends 14% of its GDP (and it is growing), which is the biggest chunk in the world.

Figure 4. Aging Japanese population: past and future

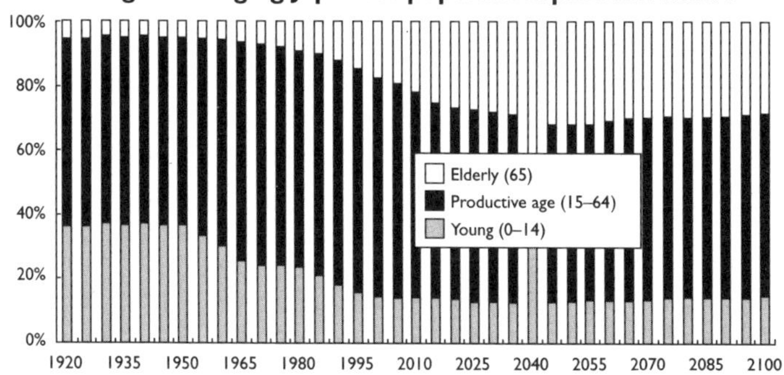

According to the MHLW, unless drastic changes are made, the amount required to fund Japan's healthcare system will increase, officially, to a staggering $800 billion per year. This could push the *actual* level of healthcare expenditure to over 20% of Japan's GDP, an amount unprecedented and probably unsustainable.

Figure 5. Health care expenditure as a percentage of Gross Domestic Product (1960–99)

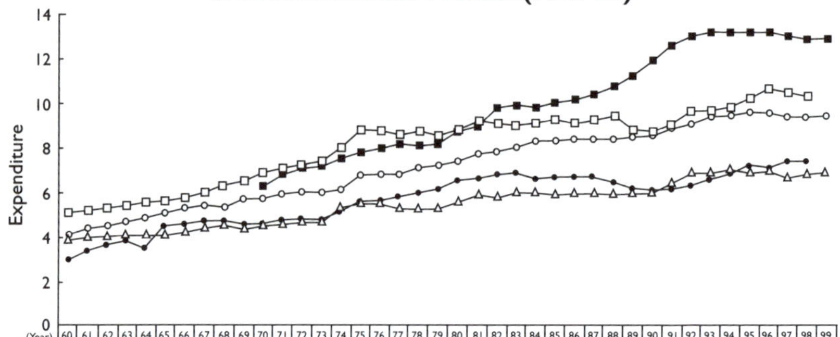

(Year)	60	61	62	63	64	65	66	67	68	69	70	71	72	73	74	75	76	77	78	79
Japan	3.0	3.4	3.6	3.9	3.3	4.5	4.6	4.7	4.7	4.6	4.6	4.7	4.8	4.7	5.1	5.6	5.6	5.8	6.0	6.1
US	5.1	5.2	5.3	5.4	5.6	5.6	5.7	6.0	6.3	6.5	6.9	7.1	7.2	7.2	7.3	7.8	8.0	8.2	8.1	8.2
UK	3.9	4.0	4.0	4.1	4.1	4.1	4.2	4.4	4.5	4.4	4.5	4.6	4.7	4.7	5.3	5.5	5.5	5.3	5.3	5.3
Germany											6.1	6.8	7.1	7.4	8.0	8.8	8.7	8.6	8.7	8.5
France	4.1	4.4	4.5	4.7	4.9	5.1	5.3	5.4	5.3	5.7	5.7	5.9	6.0	6.0	6.1	6.8	6.8	6.8	7.1	7.2

(Year)	80	81	82	83	84	85	86	87	88	89	90	91	92	93	94	95	96	97	98	99
Japan	6.5	6.6	6.8	6.9	6.6	6.7	6.7	6.7	6.4	6.2	6.1	6.1	6.1	6.6	6.9	7.2	7.1	7.4	7.4	
US	8.7	9.0	9.8	9.9	9.8	10	10	10	10	11	11	12	13	13	13	13	13	13	12	13
UK	5.6	5.9	5.8	6.0	6.0	5.9	5.9	6.0	5.9	5.9	6.0	6.4	6.9	6.9	7.0	6.9	7.0	6.7	6.8	6.9
Germany	8.8	9.2	9.1	9.0	9.1	9.3	9.1	9.2	9.4	8.8	8.7	9.1	9.7	9.7	9.8	10	10	10	10	
France	7.4	7.7	7.8	8.0	8.3	8.3	8.4	8.4	8.4	8.5	8.6	8.9	9.1	9.5	9.4	9.6	9.6	9.4	9.4	9.4

Japan — US — UK — Germany — France

Source: 'OECD Health Data 2001' Total expenditure on health – % gross domestic product

PERSPECTIVE A:

SPENDING ON HEALTHCARE IS GOOD FOR THE ECONOMY

Spending 20% of our GDP or more on healthcare is not necessarily a bad thing. In fact, if the money is used properly, it can be used to employ massive numbers of people or develop technologies that can be sold throughout the world. Most importantly, that kind of spending could boost the economy as a whole. Besides the money, we cannot ignore our obligation to care for the elderly – who happen to be the generation that built modern Japan out of the post-war ashes. We should not even think about rationing healthcare to these individuals who set up the system to begin with. Nor can we ignore out next generation, who will also require proper levels of care so that they can maintain our high levels of productivity with fewer numbers of people. We should find ways to turn this difficult situation into an advantage.

PERSPECTIVE B:

HEALTHCARE COULD SINK THE ENTIRE ECONOMY

No society in history has ever been faced with a predicament like this. In 15 to 20 years one-fourth of the population will be dependant upon the revenue coming from roughly another one-fourth's taxes. Without a drastic change in the functionality and economics of the current system, it could cripple the next generation of workers with an unbearable tax burden. This tax situation could further degrade Japan's overall individual and corporate competitiveness to the point where we would no longer be a competitive industrialized nation. Healthcare expenditures must be reined in and redistributed as soon as possible or we may face financial ruin.

3. THE FINANCIAL HEALTH OF HOSPITALS

The statistics speak for themselves. Seventy percent of all hospitals in Japan are operating in the red. The question is: can the system survive this growing trend?

Figure 6. Percentage of hospitals operating at a loss (June 2000)

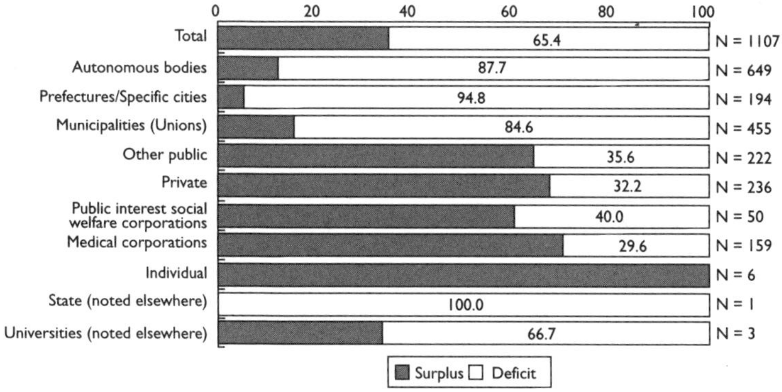

Source: 'The Survey on Actual Conditions Regarding Access to Japan, Health Care Services, July 2002,' JETRO

PERSPECTIVE A:

HOSPITALS ARE GOING BROKE. OF COURSE – HEALTHCARE IS NOT FOR PROFIT!

According to official tax data, some 70% to 80% of all hospitals in Japan are losing money. This fact alone clearly demonstrates that there is no excessive profit-taking and that, in many cases, the system is under great financial strain. The only way to remedy the situation is to do one or more of several things: a) decrease the number of beds to limit supply and increase bed utilization and efficiency; b) increase the price of procedures so that healthcare facilities can earn more; or c) decrease the cost of the goods and services used by hospitals so they can reduce their expenses. There are no other ways for the system's stakeholders, namely the hospitals and clinics, to become financially solvent.

Figure 7. Change in the number of hospitals

Source: Ministry of Health, Labour and Welfare, Minister's Secretariat, Statistics and Information Dept., 'Medical Facilities (Trend and States) Survey/Hospital Report'

PERSPECTIVE B:

THERE IS PLENTY OF MONEY; THERE IS SIMPLY A LOT OF SKIMMING EXCESS FUNDS TO AVOID PROFIT

Unlike most businesses around the world, Japanese hospitals consider it almost sinful to make a profit. When hospital managers say their hospitals are operating in the red, they do so with a sigh, but also with an air of saintly pride since this somehow implies that all their money is being spent on patient care. There is no profiteering off the backs of the sick here, they seem to be saying. In actual fact, current Japanese tax law provides no business incentive for hospitals to declare profits unless, of course, they simply want to pay taxes. From the perspective of hospital owners, it makes much more sense to give yourself perks, pay yourself a bonus or arrange other intricate ways to skim funds in order to ensure negative profitability. What's more, by taking this route, there is even the added bonus of bragging rights about your hospital's poor financial state.

The most common way to profit and still stay in the red is to form what is referred to in the shadow world as 'tunnel companies,' which are firms set-up to provide specific services to a specific hospital. The tunnel company will buy goods or services from a supplier and then resell them to the hospital. The profits of these tunnel companies go to the hospital owner's favorite charity – namely, themselves. There are numerous examples of this ranging from laundry services, sale of eyeglasses, and hospital vending machines, to parking lots, auto rentals, computer services and technical consulting services – just to name a few.

Some of the worst offenders are the public hospitals, however, even though there may not be any skimming or sheltering of funds. For public hospitals there is a general feeling that they are sitting on a bottomless pit of money (the national treasury) which leads simply to bad operating practices and bad business decisions in line with most financially irresponsible and unaccountable government bureaucracies.

Figure 8. Healthcare spending breakdown

	Fiscal 1999	
	Estimated amount (billion yen)	Component percentage (%)
National medical fees	309,377	100.0
Public	101,759	32.9
National	76,957	24.9
Public	24,801	8.0
Insurance premiums	162,253	52.5
Business owner	69,520	22.5
Employees	92,724	30.0
Other	45,325	14.7
Patient-funded	45,039	14.6

4. THE PRODUCTIVITY OF THE SYSTEM

Because there are so few reliable statistics available, it is hard to quantify or compare the productivity of Japan's healthcare system. In any case, let us now take a look at what figures do exist. For example, we know that the average length of stay in a hospital in Japan is twenty-seven days versus three days in the US and about six days in Western Europe. We also know that there are about 1,700,000 available hospital beds in Japan compared to about 900,000 in the US – even though the United States has twice the population. We also know that about 30% of Japan's total healthcare bill is for pharmaceuticals compared to just 11% in the United States. Drug spending in Western Europe is similar to that of the States. These numbers strongly suggest that the Japanese system lags behind other industrialized countries in the productivity of its healthcare delivery.

Conversely, however, other figures tell a different story. As already mentioned, Japan has the lowest infant mortality rates and the highest longevity in the world. We also know that nearly 100% of the popula-

Figure 9. Inpatient beds per 1,000 population (1960–99)

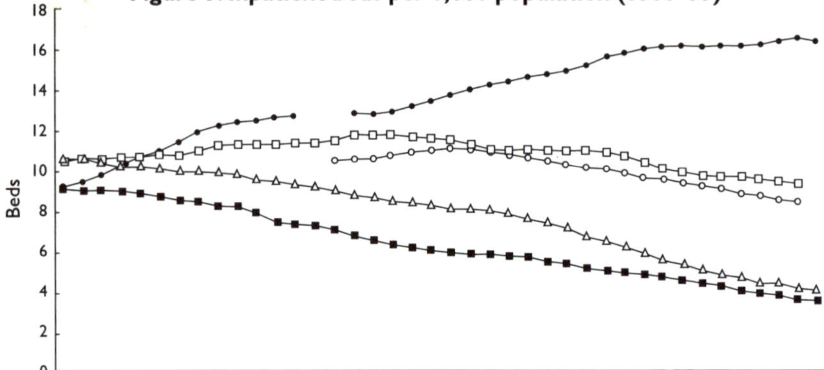

(Year)	60	61	62	63	64	65	66	67	68	69	70	71	72	73	74	75	76	77	78	79
Japan	9.0	9.4	9.8	10	10	10	11	11	12	12	12	12	12			12	12	12	13	13
US	9.2	9.1	9.1	9.0	8.9	8.8	8.6	8.5	8.3	8.2	7.9	7.5	7.4	7.3	7.1	6.8	6.6	6.4	6.2	6.1
UK	10	10	10	10	10	10	10	10	9.9	9.8	9.6	9.3	9.1	9.2	9.0	8.8	8.7	8.5	8.4	8.3
Germany	10	10	10	10	10	10	10	11	11	11	11	11	11	11	11	11	11	11	11	11
France			9.6					9.8					9.2		10	10	10	10	10	11

(Year)	80	81	82	83	84	85	86	87	88	89	90	91	92	93	94	95	96	97	98	99
Japan	13	14	14	14	14	14	14	15	15	15	16	16	16	16	16	16	16	16	16	16
US	6.0	5.9	5.9	5.8	5.7	5.5	5.4	5.2	5.1	5.0	4.9	4.8	4.6	4.5	4.3	4.1	4.0	3.9	3.7	3.6
UK	8.1	8.1	8.0	7.9	7.6	7.4	7.2	6.8	6.5	6.2	5.9	5.6	5.4	5.1	4.8	4.7	4.3	4.4	4.2	4.1
Germany	11	11	11	11	11	11	11	11	10	10	10	10	9.9	9.7	9.7	9.7	9.6	9.4	9.3	
France	11	11	11	10	10	10	10	10	10	9.9	9.7	9.6	9.4	9.3	9.1	8.9	8.8	8.6	8.5	

Japan US UK Germany France

tion are insured for basic care. The ratio of physicians to population (240,000 licensed doctors to 127 million people) is also as good as or better than in many other countries – all of which indicate better than expected productivity. As with everything related to Japanese healthcare, it seems, any conclusions to be drawn about productivity depend more on perspective than anything else.

Figure 10. Salaries of healthcare staff

(Unit yen)

Monthly salary by occupation		Salary by type of payment		Salary by type of employment	
1st class helper	190,018	Full-time employee (monthly salary)	226,677	Monthly pay	224,726
2nd class helper	130,736	Full-time employee (hourly salary)	1,021	Daily pay	8,183
3rd class helper	116,434	Short-time employee (hourly salary)	1,022	Hourly pay	1,203
Care manager	276,057	Part-time employee (hourly salary)	1,329		

Source: National Personnel Authority, Bureau of Remuneration and Employment Environment, 'State of Salaries in the Private Sector (2001)' (salaries as of April 2001; includes overtime pay')

PERSPECTIVE A:
JAPANESE HEALTHCARE IS VERY PRODUCTIVE

Of course the Japanese healthcare delivery system is one of the most efficient and most productive in the world. It is a fact that Japan spends only 8% of its GDP on healthcare. Moreover, all Japanese people have full and fair access to the system, particularly when compared to the United States, which spends nearly 14% of its GDP on healthcare but still has some 30 million people outside the system. Physicians in Japan see an average of 60 to 70 patients per day and make a fraction of what their American counterparts earn. Yet these US physicians see only 10 to 20 patients a day.

In Japan we use the latest technology efficiently and extensively. Take medical imaging, for example. When compared to the US or Western Europe on a yearly basis, Japan does nearly double the number of MRI and CAT Scan tests. Japan has approved nearly 100 blood cancer markers for early cancer diagnosis whereas only five or six of these markers are used in Western countries. Even in the area of pharmaceutical delivery, Japan seems more efficient. Japanese patients can go directly to their doctor for prescriptions. In the US, by contrast, patients are forced to use outside pharmacies and receive drugs from non-physicians who have never even examined them.

No one needs an appointment at a Japanese hospital. This system promotes the most efficient use of physician time by facilitating a rapid diagnosis by a generalist and a nearly immediate referral to a specialist – usually the very same day. In the West, a patient has to wait weeks for an appointment, then weeks again to see a specialist. This gap between appointments clearly spells poor overall productivity and disappointing levels of patient care.

Figure 11. Per capita health expenditure (PPP, $, 1999)

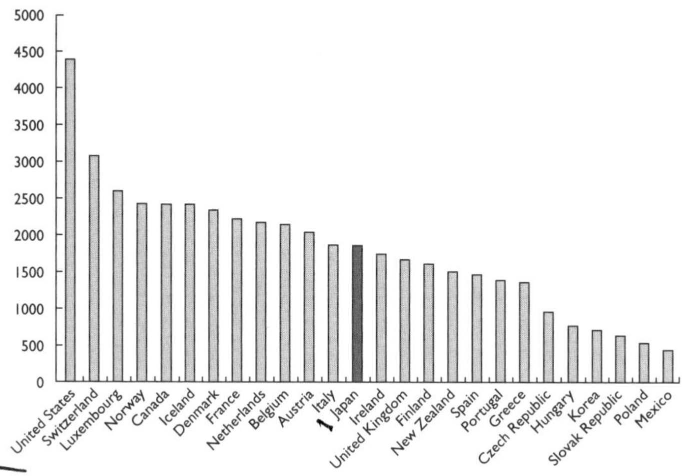

Source: 'Public Health of Japan 2002', Japan Public Health Association

Because of the large number of hospital beds, the relative cost is much lower than in the West. This allows Japanese physicians to keep more patients in hospital longer, providing regular daily care more efficiently and more cheaply. It also allows doctors to monitor their patients' lifestyles and living environment which ensures proper nutrition and lowered stress levels. This practice also allows patients to rest thoroughly, allowing their bodies and minds to heal so that they can truly become healthy again.

PERSPECTIVE B:

THE PRODUCTIVITY OF JAPANESE HEALTHCARE IS POOR

If productivity is defined as activity, Japan certainly has a highly productive system. If you define productivity as the benefits or results accrued from any given unit of activity, however, the story is very different.

There is no question that Japanese healthcare involves a great deal of activity. Lots of doctors see lots of patients. Lots of patients spend lots of time interacting with the system and these same patients spend unprecedented amounts of time in hospital. But the question is: how good is the quality of these interactions? It is a well-known fact that physicians in Japan only spend short amounts of time with patients. Can doctors actually accurately diagnosis and treat a patient in this amount of time? Can a Japanese physician do in three to five minutes what a Western physician takes fifteen to do? Although feasible, it is unlikely, particularly since Japanese physician education tends to be poor and there are very few requirements for doctors in Japan to maintain ongoing education or testing. Furthermore, if you note that there is no effective system of checks and balances for the medical practices that do take place, it is even more unlikely.

Although it may be possible to try and scientifically quantify and compare the relative productivity of different medical systems, this process requires transparency, something sorely lacking in Japan's medical world. Interestingly though, exposing the flaws and the real productivity of the current system is in fact the first step in improving productivity.

We can argue about the productivity of any medical system ad nauseam. What needs to happen, however, is: a) the creation of more transparency concerning the amount of time and money spent at the point of care delivery; b) the use of information technology to help understand which facilities deliver the most effective care; and c) to provide incentives to the good hospitals and disincentives for the bad ones. While such actions seem like a relatively straightforward approach to the productivity issue, they are also unlikely to occur because most of the current system's stakeholders are blindly patting themselves on the back about what a wonderfully productive system is already in place. The MHLW and the JMA are particularly guilty of this complacency. Neither of these organizations have any incentive to provide the level of transparency necessary to allow productivity to be analyzed and for such data to be used to improve the system.

If those involved in Japan's healthcare system are so confident about the high levels of productivity, they should allow it to be accurately assessed and quantified. Perhaps, one wonders, is it possible they have something to hide?

5. THE LENGTH OF HOSPITAL STAYS

In 1990, the average length of stay in a hospital in Japan was approximately 42 days. This number is now down to about 27 days. This

Figure 12. Average length of hospital stay in Japan

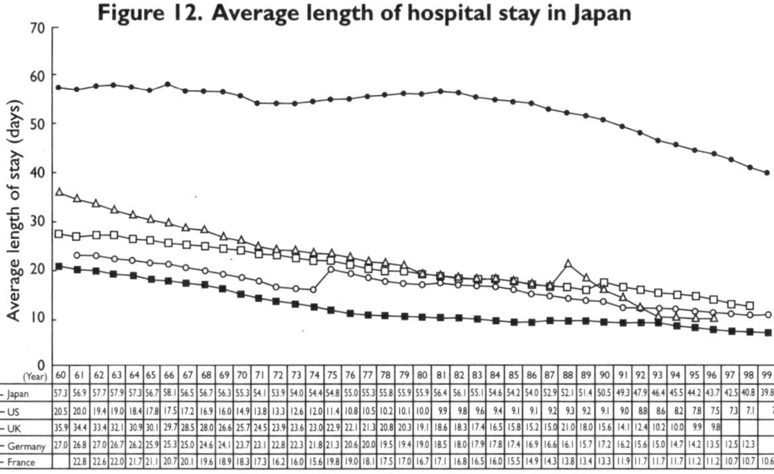

(Year)	60	61	62	63	64	65	66	67	68	69	70	71	72	73	74	75	76	77	78	79
Japan	57.3	56.9	57.7	57.9	57.3	56.7	58.1	56.5	56.7	56.3	55.3	54.1	53.9	54.0	54.4	54.8	55.0	55.3	55.8	55.9
US	20.5	20.0	19.4	19.0	18.4	17.8	17.5	17.2	16.9	16.0	14.9	13.8	13.3	12.6	12.0	11.4	10.8	10.5	10.2	10.1
UK	35.9	34.4	33.4	32.1	30.9	30.1	29.7	28.5	28.0	26.6	25.7	24.5	23.9	23.6	23.0	22.9	22.1	21.3	20.8	20.3
Germany	27.0	26.8	27.0	26.7	26.2	25.9	25.3	25.0	24.6	24.1	23.7	23.1	22.8	22.3	21.8	21.3	20.6	20.0	19.5	19.4
France		22.8	22.6	22.0	21.7	21.1	20.7	20.1	19.6	18.9	18.3	17.3	16.2	16.0	15.6	19.8	19.0	18.1	17.5	17.0

(Year)	80	81	82	83	84	85	86	87	88	89	90	91	92	93	94	95	96	97	98	99
Japan	55.9	56.4	56.1	55.1	54.6	54.2	54.0	52.9	52.1	51.4	50.5	49.3	47.9	46.4	45.5	44.2	43.7	42.5	40.8	39.8
US	10.0	9.9	9.8	9.6	9.4	9.1	9.1	9.2	9.3	9.2	9.1	9.0	8.8	8.6	8.2	7.8	7.5	7.3	7.1	7
UK	19.1	18.6	18.3	17.4	16.5	15.8	15.2	15.0	21.0	18.0	15.6	14.1	12.4	10.2	10.0	9.9	9.8			
Germany	19.0	18.5	18.0	17.9	17.8	17.4	16.9	16.6	16.1	15.7	17.2	16.2	15.6	15.0	14.7	14.2	13.5	12.5	12.3	
France	16.7	17.1	16.8	16.5	16.0	15.5	14.9	14.3	13.8	13.4	13.3	11.9	11.7	11.7	11.7	11.2	11.2	10.7	10.7	10.6

Japan — US — UK — Germany — France

Source: OECD Health Data 2001

compares with three to four days in the United States and five to eight days in Western Europe.

PERSPECTIVE A:

LONGER HOSPITALS STAYS ARE STRUCTURALLY NECESSARY IN JAPAN

Probably, most Japanese people believe that, although independent, their membership in society at large is an important part of their identity. Traditionally, Japanese people have been taught that the relationship between society and the individual is one of mutual interdependence. If an individual cooperates with the general goals of society and is a useful citizen, this scenario goes, he or she is nurtured and rewarded over time as a humble though worthy member of the paternalistic group. Recent economic trends, however, have upset the apple cart and made it harder for society to fulfill these obligations to its members. Notwithstanding these recent events, however, most Japanese people still feel the need to be nurtured and cared for, a characteristic that has, above all others, resulted in traditionally long hospital stays.

Figure 13. International comparison of average length of hospital stay in 1996

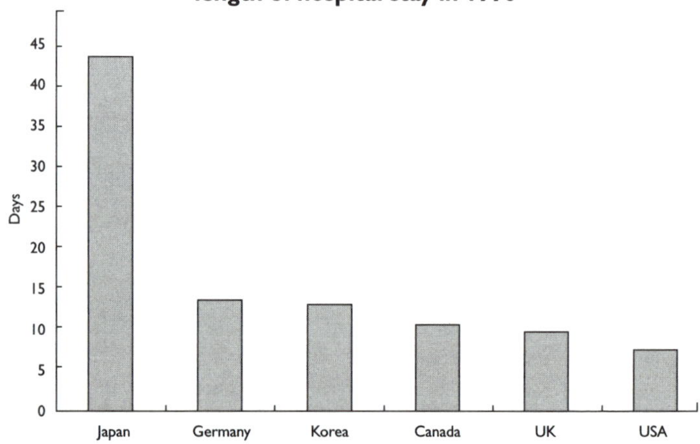

Some very basic structural elements have also contributed to long hospital stays in Japan. One such element is a public infrastructure which is essentially unfriendly and unsuited to the disabled. Houses are small and public transportation systems are not designed for people who have difficulty getting around. For those with major illnesses or other physical challenges in Japan, life is difficult. Getting to hospitals for treatment can be a major trial and even home is not necessarily a stress-free environment due to cramped quarters inhospitable to wheelchairs or other support equipment.

Another point that needs to be addressed with regard to long hospital stays is that the ratio of hospital staff to patients is significantly lower than in Western countries. As a result, everything occurs slower than in environments with higher staff-to-patient ratios. This fact needs to be taken into account when calculating the economic benefits of shorter hospital stays. How much more does increased staffing cost vs. the economic benefit of shorter hospital stays?

Most people do not understand the economics of hospital stays. But, one thing is clear: that a rapid movement toward short, Western-style length of stays will hurt a great many patients – especially those older people without an adequate support system at home and who fully believed in Japan as a nurturing society. Perhaps over time the younger generations can adapt and accept this concept, but, in the meantime, it is essential that we do not move too fast.

PERSPECTIVE B:

LONG HOSPITAL STAYS IN JAPAN ARE SIMPLY A MATTER OF HOSPITALS WANTING TO MAKE MORE MONEY

Many will find little merit to the idea that Japanese have a cultural need to spend extended time in the hospital when compared with their Western counterparts. Lengthy hospital stays in Japan are simply about making money. Under the current fee-for-service system, a hospitalized patient represents a reservoir of ready cash for the institution where they are staying. Granted, a great many patients and their families may find it convenient to stay in hospital in comparison to the rigors of outpatient treatment. But, the simple truth is that a great many other patients find that long mandatory hospital stays are nothing more than another burden on their families, employers, and social lives.

Let's face it: the Japanese body is no different than a Western one. So it is clearly safe to say that, medically speaking, a Japanese patient should be able to recover just as quickly as someone from any other modern, industrialized country. The only rational conclusion one can draw, therefore, is that hospital stays which are 500% longer in one place than another are medically unnecessary. Financial responsibility also dictates that patients should be discharged as soon they have achieved a reasonable level of recovery.

The last point is perhaps the most important. The fact is that the longer patients remain in hospital, the more likely they are to contract a hospital-acquired illness which could lead to severe complications or even death. Think about it: what hospitals do is group together sick people, many with already-compromised immune systems. Furthermore, nearly all of these patients are being treated with antibiotics, creating a ready environment for super-bugs which will have access to hundreds of susceptible potential hosts. If we are trying to create a way for bacteria to destroy mankind, the modern hospital is the place to do so. Keeping patients in such a place for as long as possible purely to satisfy financial needs is both a crime against the patients and against society at large.

Japan must do everything in its power to shorten hospital stays. The imperative to do so is economically, medically, and socially obligatory. To accomplish this goal, the current fee-for-service system must be abandoned in favor of a prospective payment system that pays a certain amount for a particular diagnosis and has capitated fees for treatment. For patients that lack a home support system during their convalescence period, nursing homes, not hospitals, are the answer.

6. PHARMACEUTICAL USE

Japan spends a significantly greater percentage of its healthcare budget on drugs than do other industrialized countries. Ten years ago in the mid-1990s nearly 30% of healthcare expenses were spent on pharmaceuticals. After implementing actions to curb drug spending, this number is now closer to 20%. which compares to the 9% to 12% in other industrialized countries. Interestingly enough, many stakeholders still quote the 30% figure, which is reflected in the perspectives taken by such people and/or institutions. It is generally believed that the reason why pharmaceutical usage is so high stems from a combination of factors. These factors include a historical connection with herbal cures, the fact that the selling of drugs has been a traditional source of physician income, and that there are a large number of highly competitive companies pushing doctors to prescribe more of their products. Another frequently cited reason is that patients want to receive drugs when they visit the doctor and not after; this conventional wisdom postulates that the more drugs a physician prescribes, the greater the value of a visit to the doctor in the eyes of patients.

The government has taken major steps to decrease pharmaceutical use. The most significant move was to remove the unofficial margin that doctors received for selling drugs. In addition, reimbursement rates have been decreasing steadily. Additionally, products that do not show significant efficacy are not being approved for sale and, when they are, they are being placed in equivalent categories at lower prices. The government is even implementing foreign reference pricing as a way of combating rising pharmaceutical costs. Despite these efforts, the pharmaceutical market – along with the age of the Japanese population – continues to spiral upward.

Some see high pharmaceutical usage in Japan as the single biggest area for potential cost savings. Others, however, see it as a unique and beneficial medical practice that leads to less intrusive therapies and drastically decreases overall care costs.

PERSPECTIVE A:

JAPANESE PHARMACEUTICAL USAGE IS NOT ONLY RATIONAL, IT IS A UNIQUELY JAPANESE PRACTICE THAT INCREASES BOTH THE QUALITY AND THE COST OF ADMINISTRATING HEALTHCARE

Hard facts clearly support the statement that Japan is one of the healthiest countries in the world. The high use of pharmaceutical products is a contributing factor to this success. If patients are being simultaneously treated for their symptoms and the diseases causing the symptoms on an ongoing basis, proponents of drug treatment contend that doing so decreases the need for more interventionist therapies. Such a policy minimizes patient care demands and helps keep costs down. Successful examples of this treatment style include therapies for hypertension, diabetes, liver disease, anemia, rheumatism, and chronic constipation. Without long-term ongoing drug therapy, all the problems mentioned above can lead to even more severe medical problems. Japan's national healthcare system helps insure these types of patients have access to the appropriate medicines, significantly decreasing morbidity and mortality rates among these patients.

There are other reasons why using drugs decreases the need for expensive, dangerous, and highly invasive therapies such as surgery. First of all, drug products are an important link between patients and doctors. Let us look at the example of a hypertensive patient placed on drug therapy who needs this drug to keep his blood pressure under control. Under Japanese law, this patient can only receive a maximum 28-day drug supply which means there is continual contact between patient and doctor. As a result, the doctor can keep a keen eye both on the primary complaints as well as on any other problems that arise. Without this pharmaceutical link, physicians may only see patients once a year or less, which is another good reason why physicians should dispense drugs.

Traditionally, Western cultures have favored more interventionist types of therapies while Eastern cultures have tended more towards less intrusive treatments. The reasons for this division are not totally clear, but it probably relates to the idea that Eastern cultures prefer a more holistic approach to medicine where a 'cure' may not be obviously connected to treatment. From a Western standpoint, this lack of clear connection between treatment and patient condition can be hard to accept.

There is no question that many of the advances in modern healthcare have resulted from pharmaceutical industry innovations. For such innovations to continue, drug companies must have robust sales so that R&D can be adequately funded. A decrease in drug sales could well mean a decrease in new products which have the potential to help patients easily and effectively without the need for expensive and intrusive procedures.

Many people point to the profit motive as the reason we use so many pharmaceutical products. Refuting this argument is the fact that, despite the recent elimination of the official profit margin given to physicians, we have not seen a marked decrease in the use of these products. This seems to illustrate that the profit motive is not a significant factor.

Yes, Japan does spend a greater percentage of its healthcare budget on drugs than other countries. If traditional Chinese herbs were included in these figures, in fact, the percentage would be even higher than official statistics indicate. But, to try and balance the financial woes of the healthcare system by cutting back on pharmaceutical usage may well be reducing one of the very factors that makes Japanese healthcare as successful as it is.

PERSPECTIVE B:

DRUG USAGE IN JAPAN IS UTTERLY IRRATIONAL. IT COSTS THE SYSTEM TOO MUCH MONEY AND MAY BE DETRIMENTAL TO THE OVERALL QUALITY OF CARE

There are many reasons why Japan overuses pharmaceutical products. First, patients expect drugs when visiting the doctor and feel unsatisfied without them. Second, doctors have been taught that prescribing drugs is good for patients. But the third and biggest reason for Japan's rampant drug use is that a lot of people make money by doing so. Period.

Doctors make money by giving drugs to patients. Pharmaceutical wholesalers make money selling drugs to doctors. Pharmaceutical manufacturers make money selling drugs to wholesalers. And, politicians make money directly through political donations from pharmaceutical companies, and indirectly from money donated to them by the JMA, a great deal of which, directly or indirectly, comes from pharmaceutical companies.

Drugs also keep patients coming back to doctors, thus generating more billing opportunities. Under Japanese law, total dosages are limited to 28 days at one dispensation. Most doctors give only 14 days' worth, and there are no refills. This means that a hypertensive patient for example, will need to go to the doctor's office at least once per month for the rest of his or her life, generating fees for each visit. As any Japanese physician running a clinic could tell you – if they were candid enough – the key to making money is to get a critical mass of patients dependent on drugs.

Aside from the productivity loss in the workforce caused by these drug-dispensing practices, they can also have negative medical impact in some cases. The single biggest example of this is antibiotics. Antibiotics are given so readily by physicians that Japan has become an epicenter for the development of resistant bacteria strains. Some of these drugs, when taken over long periods of time, can also have other adverse effects, most notably on the liver and kidneys.

These days, however, even patients have begun to question the amount and usefulness of the drugs they are prescribed. Now that patients are paying up to 30% of the bill themselves, there is a growing trend to question doctors on the need for some prescriptions.

Thirty percent of healthcare money in Japan is spent on pharmaceutical products. If this percentage could be reduced to perhaps 15% – still above the industrialized world's norm – this could yield savings of over $50 billion per year. Within the current system, no other single saving comes close to matching this figure. Achieving this saving is simple: eliminate the financial incentive for doctors selling drugs to patients. To do so, the dispensing and prescribing functions must be separated. Also, strict penalties must be imposed on drug dispensers or pharmaceutical companies who give money or other benefits to doctors prescribing a certain kind of drug. Expanding the current prospective payment (DPC) system to the entire marketplace – and including pharmaceutical usage in the DPC coding – would also help stop physicians from over-prescribing.

7. MEDICAL TECHNOLOGY AND HOW IT IS USED

Japan boasts the use of some of the most advanced technologies in the world. Nearly all technologies that have been made available in the West ultimately find their way to Japan. The effectiveness of how these technologies are evaluated and used is a matter of significant debate, however, and once again we find several groups with very different perspectives.

PERSPECTIVE A:
TECHNOLOGY IS USED INEFFECTIVELY

In the past, getting new technologies approved and placed within the reimbursement scheme was fairly simple. Recently, however, these new technologies have not been viewed in light of patient benefit, but rather in terms of their cost to the publicly funded system. The Japanese public is being denied the newest drugs, diagnostic procedures, and equipment because the government considers them too costly. Although it is understandable that every system must accommodate certain financial realities to remain viable, what has not been considered is that many of these technologies can create efficiencies leading to cheaper overall patient care when used effectively and appropriately. Moreover, since these new technologies are simply so much better than the old ones, they simply have to be adopted on humanitarian grounds.

The next issue relating to the use of technology is the way in which the medical profession adopts these technologies. Because there is no mandatory continuing medical education system, specialty board examinations, or any significant threat of malpractice against physicians, it is questionable if most medical professionals can effectively use the latest technology.

Figure 14. % of general hospitals owning high-tech equipment

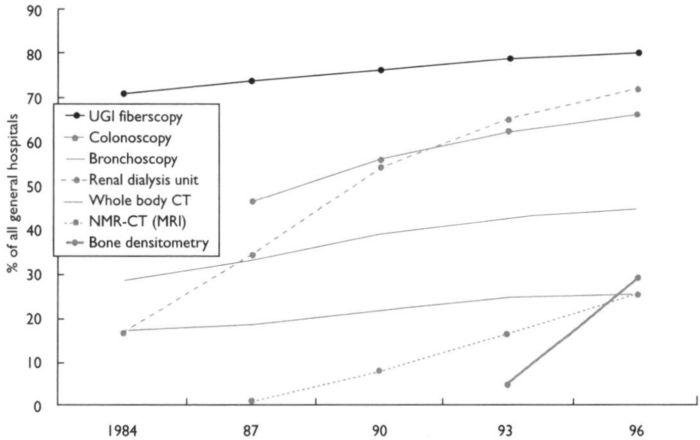

Source: 'Public Health of Japan 2002,' Japan Public Health Association

In the good old days, when technologies were easily approved in the cash-rich 1980s, a number of technologies were adopted for use in Japan. At that time, the representative technologies were usually safe but often ineffective. There are still hundreds of these kinds of products in use today, needlessly draining cash from the healthcare coffers. These ineffectual technologies need to be filtered and removed from hospital shelves. The resulting savings should be used for newer, more advanced methods capable of improving patient care, and in some cases, reducing costs.

The last word on the use of technology is that, in the end, the successful use of advanced methods and machinery costs more. Because these technologies can help people live longer, healthier lives, they prolong the inevitable – mainly for the age group that puts the biggest financial strain on the system: the elderly. From a purely financial view, denying these technologies to the Japanese population makes a kind of twisted sense. But, as a democracy Japan must invite the general public into this debate and ultimately choose how to spend their money.

A system needs to be created that can evaluate the cost/benefit effectiveness of new technologies. To help ensure that they are used productively and knowledgeably, the medical profession needs to be held accountable. If the denial of technologies by the government is the order of the day, the Japanese people need to be allowed to voice their opinion as to this policy's appropriateness.

PERSPECTIVE B:

TECHNOLOGY IS USED EFFECTIVELY

Japanese people tend to be pragmatic when it comes to technology use in healthcare. Although not necessarily official policy, the behavior of those in charge clearly indicates a preference for technologies designed to diagnose disease states early and facilitate early, less invasive – and less expensive – treatment. Diagnostic imaging is one good example of this unstated policy in action. Japan has more MRI and CAT Scan equipment per capita than any other industrialized country and, despite its great cost, the technologies were imported because they matched the above philosophy.

Another interesting move by Japan has been to let other countries use and gain experience with other drugs and technologies before adopting them in Japan. While this approach may appear selfish, it has been very useful in screening out seemingly promising technologies that turned out to be ineffective, costly, or dangerous.

What is poorly understood about technology policy in Japan is that the priority is to spend money on human resources first. The philosophy of the system, it seems, is to ensure that there are enough qualified physicians, pharmacists, nurses, dentists, and other healthcare providers. Technology, on the other hand, is seen as a less important and somewhat useful tool for these medical professionals. When Japan has been faced with either spending its limited resources on people or technology, it has consistently made the brave decision to support the three million dedicated professionals who are the backbone of healthcare.

To summarize, Japan has a unique philosophy toward the use of technologies. We do not spend resources, as a rule, on heroic and expensive treatments that have a lower probability of success. Rather, we spend these resourses on diagnoses and treatments that have the best chance of achieving cost-effective success. Japan also has a tendency to give technologies time to mature so productivity and cost-effectiveness can be better understood. Lastly, Japan would rather spend money on people than on technology wherever possible. It is the quantity and the quality of the contact between patient and caregiver that ultimately provides the most value in the majority of cases.

8. PHYSICIAN EDUCATION

There are 80 university hospitals in Japan and roughly 8,000 physicians graduate from this system each year. Students begin their medical education system directly out of high school and, after six years of higher education, students sit for a paper-based examination. If they pass they are licensed for life as a medical doctor. As of 2004, a two-year residency period will be added to the course work on a voluntary basis.

After medical school, there are no requirements for further education. Nor is there any further testing. There are, however, hundreds of physician education and research organizations called *gakkai*. These mostly volunteer organizations can be either broad in scope (e.g., internal medicine), or very specific, perhaps dealing with only a single disease such as, say, diabetes. Many of these organizations have thou-

Figure 15. Practicing physicians per 1,000 population (1960–99)

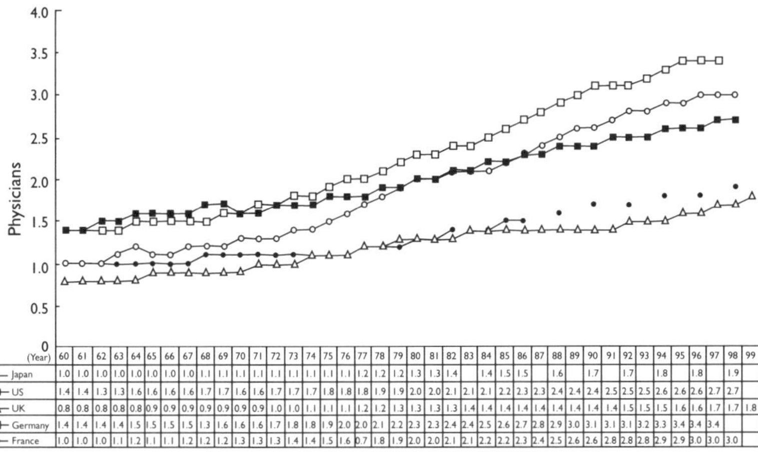

(Year)	60	61	62	63	64	65	66	67	68	69	70	71	72	73	74	75	76	77	78	79
Japan	1.0	1.0	1.0	1.0	1.0	1.0	1.0	1.0	1.1	1.1	1.1	1.1	1.1	1.1	1.1	1.1	1.1	1.2	1.2	1.2
US	1.4	1.4	1.3	1.3	1.6	1.6	1.6	1.6	1.7	1.7	1.6	1.6	1.7	1.7	1.7	1.8	1.8	1.8	1.9	1.9
UK	0.8	0.8	0.8	0.8	0.8	0.9	0.9	0.9	0.9	0.9	0.9	0.9	1.0	1.0	1.1	1.1	1.1	1.2	1.2	1.3
Germany	1.4	1.4	1.4	1.4	1.5	1.5	1.5	1.5	1.3	1.6	1.6	1.6	1.7	1.8	1.8	1.9	2.0	2.0	2.1	2.2
France	1.0	1.0	1.0	1.1	1.2	1.1	1.1	1.2	1.2	1.2	1.3	1.3	1.3	1.4	1.4	1.5	1.6	0.7	1.8	1.9

(Year)	80	81	82	83	84	85	86	87	88	89	90	91	92	93	94	95	96	97	98	99
Japan	1.3	1.3	1.4		1.4	1.5	1.5		1.6		1.7		1.7		1.8		1.8		1.9	
US	2.0	2.0	2.1	2.1	2.1	2.2	2.3	2.3	2.4	2.4	2.4	2.5	2.5	2.5	2.6	2.6	2.6	2.7	2.7	
UK	1.3	1.3	1.3	1.4	1.4	1.4	1.4	1.4	1.4	1.4	1.4	1.4	1.5	1.5	1.5	1.6	1.6	1.7	1.7	1.8
Germany	2.3	2.3	2.4	2.4	2.5	2.6	2.7	2.8	2.9	3.0	3.1	3.1	3.1	3.2	3.3	3.4	3.4	3.4		
France	2.0	2.0	2.1	2.1	2.2	2.2	2.3	2.4	2.5	2.6	2.6	2.8	2.8	2.8	2.9	2.9	3.0	3.0	3.0	

—•— Japan —■— US —△— UK —□— Germany —○— France

Source: OECD Health Data 2001, 'Practicing Physicians – Density/1000 Population'

sands of members and some of the smaller ones may have just a few. While not mandatory, a large number of doctors participate in *gakkai*, and often in more than one. The *gakkai*'s job is to provide its member with information on new advances in their specific field. Most information exchange occurs at national or regional meetings or via newsletters and/or websites.

In 2004, for the first time, the government will get involved in regulating *gakkai* and using them as a tool for monitoring specialists. If a *gakkai* chooses to become officially certified, it can issue special certification to its members allowing them to advertise. In this early attempt at regulating the post-graduate medical professional system, the MHLW has created a number of criteria that *gakkai* must comply with in order to gain the new elevated status. These requirements include a minimum of 200 members and that 60% of these members are MDs. It is also required that they have an education and credentials committee and that these committees have published policies concerning the ongoing education of their members.

Not surprisingly, some in the medical field are happy with these recent moves and what they suggest for the future while others are growing quite uncomfortable.

PERSPECTIVE A:

THE CURRENT SYSTEM OF POST-GRADUATE MEDICAL EDUCATION IS WORKING FINE. DO NOT ADD ANOTHER WASTEFUL BURDEN TO AN ALREADY OVERSTRETCHED SYSTEM

The term used to describe how a physician works is 'practicing.' A doctor practices and learns with every patient he or she sees. After graduating from medical school, young physicians have a basic foundation to work from, but their true knowledge is accrued from their daily work with the hundreds and thousands of patients they see over their career. On-the-job-training, if you will, is a long-tested and effective method for gaining and maintaining the proper amount of knowledge to practice effective medicine.

There is, of course, an ongoing need to understand advances in diagnostic and treatment practices. Currently, this role is filled by *gakkai*, company medical reps, and through government guidelines. The combination of *gakkai* meetings and information sent from *gakkai* to doctors is an effective means of ensuring that physicians remain current on advances both in general medicine and in specialty areas.

Moreover, medical advances are ultimately commercialized and are then promoted by an army of well-trained, certified medical industry representatives. Lastly, as new procedures are listed on the reimbursement schedule by the MHLW, there is a strong monetary incentive to understand these technologies and how they work. This incentive, in turn, drives doctors to study the information provided by the *gakkai* and the medical representatives.

From outside the medical profession, it is easy to say that doctors should to be required to undertake continuous study. Continuing Medical Education (CME) makes patients feel more secure and some members of the press constantly point to the lack of CME as a flaw of Japan's system. From a practical perspective, however, CME will have little real benefit. The fact is that doctors study constantly as they work. There is a good system in place to assure that information on new methods is disseminated properly. Placing an extra burden of compulsory study and testing will simply add stress to doctors' already stressful lives. Valuable time will be stolen from patients and important professional interaction.

While it may appear glamorous, being a doctor is hard work. Too many things already take up too much time. A bureaucratic system of enforced education and testing (with the axe of non-license renewal hanging over their heads) will stress the system and doctors even further and perhaps – for some – to the breaking point.

PERSPECTIVE B:

THE CURRENT MOVES TO REQUIRE POST-GRADUATE MEDICAL EDUCATION ARE TO BE APPLAUDED AND THEIR IMPLEMENTATION HASTENED

The practice of medicine is one of the most important and most complicated of human endeavors. Even through the 1960s when medical advances in both knowledge and technology occurred comparatively slowly, it was very difficult for doctors to effectively keep up with the overwhelming body of knowledge. Now that the amount of information has exponentially increased and continues to do so, it is an even more arduous task.

The life of a physician can be challenging and stressful. As human beings, it is easy to understand why some physicians, when faced with this tsunami of new information, might simply want to give up trying to take everything in. While such a feeling is understandable, however, it is equally unacceptable. Patients place their trust in doctors. The betrayal of this trust potentially carries with it the most dire of consequences – the patient's loss of life. Regardless of how tough it is for doctors, society demands that physicians study, are tested, and remain accountable for the minimum level of knowledge required to practice modern medicine. If they fail to do so, their right to practice medicine should be removed.

Some may argue that Japan's current system already accommodates post-graduate education for doctors. Unquestionably, copious amounts of information are made available to physicians through *gakkai* and medical reps. The problem, however, lies in the fact that CME as it now stands is 100% voluntary and depends entirely on the good intentions of each doctor. While no good statistics are available, the general feeling is that most doctors simply do not study enough and, as a result, many may not be truly qualified to practice.

The current steps moving doctors towards more educational requirements should be commended. All stakeholders clearly understand that the MHLW is taking such steps despite the risk of backlash by the likes of the JMA. They should be equally commended for the new residency requirements for recently graduated physicians. But, regardless of the political give and take, it simply is not happening fast enough. The following steps need to be taken as soon as possible:

1) A minimum number of documented education hours must be required for physicians to maintain their licenses. Lying about, or forging, compliance documentation must become a punishable crime.
2) To decrease the cost of education delivery, the Internet should be used more extensively for both education and testing.
3) Tests should be regularly administered to all doctors based on their specialty. These tests should focus on new advances.
4) All physician education data should be made available to the public over the Internet.

Being a doctor is a tough job. There is too much to know and not enough time to learn it all. The problem is not a lack of information. The problem is the lack of incentives for doctors to access and learn this information. The only way to ensure that physicians learn is compulsory study backed up with regular testing. Those who fail should be removed from the system. In the practice of medicine, the price for incompetence is simply too high.

9. JAPAN'S MEDICAL CULTURE

Many of Japan's fundamental cultural attributes can be traced back to the fusion of a cooperative agrarian work ethic and the strict hierarchy of the warrior, or *bushi*, class. Out of these and other complex elements grew an effective and cooperative society that gave birth to one of the most powerful economies of the twentieth century. As one might expect, these same cultural elements permeate throughout Japan's healthcare system and have deep-rooted effects on the practice of medicine and the organization of medical education and hospitals. At the same time, the overall thrust of medicine is Western-derived science. The result is a system that seems quite Western from outer appearances, but one that is also distinctively Japanese.

The most prominently Japanese part of this system is that of *senpai* and *kohai*. The *senpai* is the elder and presumably wiser while the *kohai* is younger and in need of mentoring. The system is replete with complex unwritten rules whereby the *kohai* is subservient to the *senpai* and should not show disrespect or contradict. In exchange, if the *kohai* can withstand the torment, it is the *senpai's* responsibility to ensure the *kohai's* future success, and in the strictest terms be willing to lay his life – or career – on the line. Although this stringent seniority system seems to be losing steam, it still dictates life in fields such as the military, police, martial arts, organized crime syndicates;4 and, of course, medicine.

PERSPECTIVE A:

THE MELDING OF WESTERN SCIENCE AND JAPANESE CULTURE HAS CREATED AN EFFICIENT, ALBEIT UNIQUE KIND OF HEALTHCARE DELIVERY

It takes thousands of years for a culture to evolve. Japan's culture is certainly unique, and has withstood the test of time. Moreover, Japanese cultural attributes have had a powerful impact on the practice of medicine. They affect, for example, the relationships between patient and physician, between physician and physician, and between teacher and student. In every relationship, Japanese culture demands that respect is shown to elders and that students respect their teachers. It is equally important that teachers take care of their students who demonstrate both academic promise and respect for societal rules. Simply speaking, the system is time-tested and works well.

From a Western perspective, the relationships that drive medical care may seem too informal and unstructured. From a Japanese perspective, however, this system creates a latticework of socially required checks and balances. It is the elder physician's job, for example, to ensure that the younger doctor cares properly for patients as well as learns the necessary skills so that they can, in turn, pass this knowledge on to their subordinates when the time comes. The real key is the multiplicity effect, whereby a single student can have multiple teachers, and the teachers have teachers themselves. Such a system provides an informal and highly effective network of checks and balances. It is an apprentice-system that works and mirrors other such systems in other cultures in other ages as well.

To carry this system to its logical end, it means that atop the pyramid is one all-knowing, all-powerful teacher. Such a hierarchical structure, of course, leaves the system open to criticism that some intolerable dictator can wield absolute power from such a lofty personal perch. While there is no question that this structure has led to abuses of power in the past, much more often the system avoids this problem by making these top positions honorific while the real decision-making power rests among those other senior teachers or physicians vying for the top spot. Again, this creates an effective system of checks and balances in medicine as it does in industry and government.

The other cultural attributes that create a strong Japanese healthcare system are an enviable work ethic and strong moral character developed through the *senpai/kohai* system which instills in patients a willingness to listen to and comply with doctors' orders.

No system is perfect, however, and all cultures change and evolve. Having said this, however, Japanese traditional culture has many strengths. When these strengths were combined with the study and quality implementation of Western-style science, a top-flight healthcare system emerged. It is also noteworthy that all the science utilized in Japan is not Western. Japan also extensively uses Eastern holistic and herbal medical treatments in combination with Western approaches. It is this mix of Eastern and Western cultures as well as science that has lead to the high quality – but sometimes poorly understood – medical system here in Japan.

The current trend to try and Westernize medical practices in Japan needs to be carefully thought out. The fact is that, as it stands now, the Japanese system can be very rigorous and even punishing for its participants. To force in, for example, Western-style facility accreditation or credentialing could overload the participants and the system to the breaking point. Increasing transparency is probably something that will stay with us, but it needs to be introduced and implemented carefully and slowly. It would be shame to throw away the positive contributions of the indigenous culture in a blind thrust towards Westernization.

Japanese culture combined with Western scientific methods and some Eastern doctrine has contributed to create a highly effective medical system. It will continue to evolve, but we should not be too quick to change purely for the sake of changing. The fact is that things are working pretty darn well!

PERSPECTIVE B:

CERTAIN ATTRIBUTES OF JAPANESE CULTURE RUN CONTRARY TO QUALITY MEDICAL PRACTICE AND ECONOMICS

One problem faced by medical systems throughout the world is the egos of very powerful physicians. Although we may not like to face this fact, physicians have – due to the very nature of their profession – essentially achieved demi-god status because they, literally, make life and death decisions. This fundamental fact, combined with elements of the Japanese culture, have combined to create an ineffective system lacking in accountability, transparency, and – in some cases – quality.

The basis of the problem lies in the traditional *senpai/kohai* system, whereby close-knit and cozy relationships are created between medical professionals. Unfortunately, many aspects of the *senpai/kohai* relationship run contrary to good medical practice. For example, one part of this unwritten code says that a *senpai* must cover up for a *kohai* in the case of a medical error. On the other hand, it is sacrilege for a *kohai* to even suggest that a *senpai* has made a mistake. Such blanket acceptance flies in the face of everything we know about quality management systems where it has been clearly shown that exposing and discussing problems freely and openly is one of the best opportunities for improvement. Such cases hold true not only in the hospital where the error occurred, but are also valuable to other professionals. Because of the protective nature of its medical establishment, the Japanese system misses nearly all of these opportunities for improvement, costing the system in increased morbidity and mortality as well as economically.

The *senpai/kohai* system is not the only one to blame for doctors' unwillingness to expose errors. Society at large needs to determine and identify blame when mistakes get made – especially ones that affect life and limb. Society and culture demand that someone falls on their sword to take responsibility. Accountability requires responsibility. We have seen the scapegoat syndrome in medicine many times over. Society feels vindicated when some elderly physician gets hauled off in handcuffs after several patients die of a nosocomial infection. But, the question that needs asking is: does such bloodletting solve the problem? Or does it simply force others to bury problems and mistakes deeper and deeper.

The culture of medicine in Japan also dictates that patients blindly accept the advice (orders) of their doctor. Patient compliance rates are ranked among the highest in the world. While this compliance certainly has benefits, when combined with the lack of professional oversight it means that physicians have nearly absolute power, particularly in Japan's nearly 5,000 private hospitals and 90,000 clinics. For these physicians, their only motivation in keeping up with medical advances is their own conscience. While I am sure that many, if not most, try to stay current, doctors are after all only human, and busy humans at that.

Changing such a deeply rooted culture is very difficult and will take time and effort. Failure to change, however, will make true healthcare reform difficult and ineffective. The government can do the following to alleviate the situation:

1) Promote the exposure of errors by indemnifying any participants that come forward in a timely fashion.
2) Depower the *sempai/kohai* system by giving tax incentives to hospitals that hire physicians and other medical professionals from different hospital/university groups.
3) Automatically suspend the medical license of any physician that covers up a medical error.
4) Force hospitals to adopt electronic medical record-keeping systems that will make cover-ups more difficult to hide.
5) Provide user-friendly information to patients over the Internet, and encourage patients to become involved in the diagnosis and treatment of their diseases.

While the culture will only change slowly, the aforementioned steps will have a profound impact and will greatly enhance any other healthcare reform policies that are put into place.

2 The Economic Debate

1. FEE-FOR-SERVICE VS. PROSPECTIVE PAYMENT

A fee-for-service medical system is one that reimburses hospitals and physicians directly for the services they perform. For example, if a physician diagnoses someone with a planter's wart, he or she could bill the patient (and/or the insurance company) for either the diagnosis, the treatment materials, or administering the treatment. On the other hand, in the simplest terms, in a prospective payment system a physician would get a flat fee for the diagnosis of the planter's wart and would be expected to render treatment for a predetermined flat fee.

The prospective style payment system started in the United States in the early 1980s urged on by Medicare and private insurers who were being asked to shoulder a continually growing financial burden. The American Medical Association (AMA) argued strongly against the implementation of this type of system until economic realities forced them to abandon their position. Two acronyms are commonly used to describe this system: PS (Prospective Payment System) and DRG (Diagnostic Related Groups). DRGs are groupings of disease categories that Medicare and other third-party payers use as a basis for hospital payment schedules.

The economic incentives for the two types of systems are essentially opposite in nature and substance. A fee-for-service system provides an economic incentive for maximizing medical treatment, while the prospective payment type economically encourages the most minimal medical treatment. Opponents of each system say that the prospective payment system promotes under-utilization of medical resources while the fee-for-service system overuses the same resources.

From the point of view of hospitals and physicians, a fee-for-service system is economically transparent. In contrast, a prospective payment system contains an inherent element of risk. If the cost of a treatment rendered is less than the scheduled amount, there is a windfall. On the other hand, if a treatment costs more than the scheduled amount, the healthcare facility loses.

This discussion surrounding what is now termed 'DRG/PPS' is, in principle, very simple. In practice, however, it is frustratingly complicated with complex interacting formulas for multiple diagnoses and a system of checks and balances to ensure that proper diagnoses are made and are not simply inventions to maximize reimbursement. This system also helps ensure that care is not inappropriately denied once patients have used up their allotted funds. This complex and confusing interaction of multiple and often conflicting objectives has created a bureaucratic labyrinth.

Until recently, the idea that Japan would ever adopt a DRG/PPS-type system was unthinkable. Much like their AMA counterparts in the 1970s in the United States, the JMA has fought hard and strong against such a system. But, in a surprising move, in April 2003 the MHLW introduced a DRG/PPS-type system into all of Japan's eighty national university hospitals. This system was designed to be cash neutral as a way of appeasing certain political powers but it is noteworthy in that it has not been implemented in private hospitals which are dominated by JMA members. The MHLW, wanting to avoid being

Figure 16. Percentages of profit and non-profit facilities in healthcare facilities

			Japan	US	UK	Germany	France
Hospitals[*1]	Facility percentage	For-profit	0.7%	15.1%	11.2%	19.9%	41.6%
		Private non-profit	79.1%	60.8%	4.1%	36.3%	21.4%
		National	20.1%	24.2%	84.0%	33.2%	40.0%
	Bed percentage	For-profit	0.9%	12.9%	3.8%	7.0%	19.9%
		Private non-profit	66.2%	70.7%	1.6%	35.8%	4.9%
		National	32.9%	16.4%	94.5%	50.7%	75.2%
	(Data year)		(1999)	(1999)	(2000–01)	(2000)	(1999)
Facilities for social welfare services for the elderly[*2]	Facility percentage	For-profit	0.0%	49.0%	79.7%	34.9%	–
		Private non-profit	92.7%	50.0%	13.4%	56.6%	–
		National	7.3%	–	7.0%	8.5%	–
	Bed percentage	For-profit	0.0%	–	78.2%	–	30.0%
		Private non-profit	92.5%	–	12% [*3]	–	33.0%
		National	7.5%	–	9.8% [*3]	–	37.0%
	(Data year)		(1999)	(1999–2001)	(2001)	(1999)	(1999)

Source: 'The Survey on Actual Conditions Regarding Access to Japan Health Care Services', July 2002, JETRO

tarred with the brush of the DRG/PPS name, has called the system DPC, or Diagnostic Procedure Combinations.

The debate rages on and there are, of course, many perspectives:

PERSPECTIVE A:

DPC WILL DESTROY HEALTHCARE IN JAPAN

The Japanese medical system is one of the best in the world. One of the main reasons for its success has been the ability of the central government to evaluate diagnostic and treatment methods for efficacy, safety, and cost-effectiveness. The central government has devised and implemented an ingenious scheme that promotes the use of quality medical practice by rewarding such behavior with higher reimbursements for using what is deemed best for the patient. Conversely, the system does not limit physician choices in any way and allows doctors always to do what is best for the patient regardless of reimbursement.

The current fee-for-service system ensures that each patient is given adequate treatment that is fair and equitable for all members of society. The current DPC system being proposed and that has already been partially implemented in university hospitals is going to force all hospitals to scrutinize their expenditures for all treatments. This initiative will inevitably cause the most needy patients to be deprived of necessary – and sometimes – life-saving treatment. In many cases this penny-pinching program will actually worsen patients' conditions, causing other pathologies to advance. Such a program could actually increase the overall cost of treatment.

The other thing that the prospective payment (DPC) system is going to do is force people to purchase supplementary health insurance and facilitate mixed public and private health insurance (kongyo shingyo). The result will be a multi-tiered system. The bottom rung of such a plan would go to the current public system and would be available to the working class. Other prospective payment systems would offer higher reimbursements for the same diagnosis for middle-class patients who can afford supplementary insurance. Finally, there will be a fee-for-service system available only to the rich. This stratified system is totally contrary to the basic tenets of Japanese society and to the fundamentals of the current healthcare system.

This march towards prospective payment must be stopped by any means possible. As a society, we are simply going to have to accept that we must pay more to care for our aging society rather than destroying the system that has served – and will continue to serve – our needs so very well.

PERSPECTIVE B:

DPC IS A FUNDAMENTAL ECONOMIC REALITY

Most patients would certainly prefer to be treated under a fee-for-service system. But, what has happened in Japan is a perfect example of why such a system is not rational and is fundamentally corrupt. This fee-for-service system has resulted in the longest hospital stays in the world. The reason: hospitalized patients are money-making machines as long as they remain in hospital. This fee-for-service system has resulted in 30% of the entire healthcare budget being spent on drugs. The reason: hospitals make money selling drugs. The basic fact of a fee-for-service system is that there is no incentive for anyone to perform their job efficiently and achieve positive clinical outcomes. On the contrary, all of the fiscal incentives are geared towards keeping patients sick and dependant on the system for as long as possible.

The switch to prospective payment is an economic reality. But, under the current structure and system, there is a real risk that patient care will deteriorate. Such a result would not be due to inadequacies of the system. Rather, declining patient care could be attributed to problems with the medical profession in Japan. These problems have resulted from a 'paint-by-numbers' method of practicing medicine created by a top-down reimbursement system in which the central government has tried to manage treatment choices in every single patient case. As a result, most Japanese physicians rely exclusively on this kind of guidance and are now unable to think independently. An abrupt switch to a system that requires physicians to engage in cognitive reasoning will be a disaster in more than a few cases.

The other issue is the lack of quality checks and balances for medical care professionals and the facilities in which they work. While there have been some recent advances, the system of facility inspection and accreditation is wholly inadequate. Professional certification and crediting systems are stuck in the Meiji era thanks to the *sempai-kohai* system where individual professors have all of the power to evaluate and grant credentials to medical professionals. Physicians are still licensed for life and are not required to have any ongoing training or confirmation of their competency. Lastly, there is no meaningful system whereby patients or their families can seek meaningful compensation in the case of sub-standard care.

With the fee-for-service system, the economic incentive is to over-treat patients. With the DPC system, the incentive is the opposite. For the system to work properly an adequate arrangement of checks and balances is essential.

Notwithstanding all of these challenges, the government should move aggressively to expand the prospective payment system beyond university hospitals. To ensure that quality standards are maintained, the government should offer economic incentives to those facilities and medical professionals that implement quality systems and achieve standards set by accreditation and certification bodies. A system requiring that all medical professionals be trained on an ongoing basis needs to be installed, and it needs to institute re-licensing exams for all doctors. Lastly, the government should make it easy for patients to acquire information about the poor quality of care they may receive and create methods promoting timely and adequate reimbursement to act as a form of punishment for those facilities and professionals who choose to abuse the system at the expense of patient care.

2. FOR-PROFIT OR NOT-FOR-PROFIT

The historical fact is that the Japanese healthcare system was based on an age-old network of privately-owned herbalists, where healing was based primarily on Chinese-style medicines. Until 1948, these clinics were all private and all-for-profit. After World War II, and with the introduction of available healthcare as stipulated by the new constitution, the government used strong economic incentives to bring the medical establishment into a national healthcare system. This system is based on several premises that include:

1) All hospitals, clinics, and physicians offer identical services at identical cost.
2) Those who participate in the system will do so with society in mind, and all medical corporations must be run as not-for-profit enterprises.

The Ministry of Health, Labour and Welfare used the lure of lucrative reimbursements to bring this largely independent group into the fold. They rewarded those physicians and hospitals that chose to participate in the prescribed methods, and financially disenfranchised the rest. Over time virtually the entire system was operating under the national healthcare scheme.

PERSPECTIVE A:

TO MAKE A PROFIT IN HEALTHCARE IS EVIL

To introduce a profit incentive into healthcare will lead to the demise of the entire system. The profit motive violates the social contract healthcare providers have with patients, and will disrupt, to its core, the practice of medicine. Physicians are trusted members of society. Patients come to them with their most intimate and pressing problems. This trust-based relationship is built partly on the fact that physicians have no profit motive.

All healthcare providers in Japan work at a fraction of the pay received by other skilled workers with equivalent educational backgrounds. Do you think that they would agree to work under such perverse economic conditions if they did not have the respect afforded them by society due to their status as public-minded servants? Practicing medicine is a great privilege and there should be no need for economic incentives above and beyond the basic living necessities.

The Japanese medical system is under great financial strain. To try and introduce a for- profit system will simply mean another mouth – the shareholder's – to feed. Why would anyone want to invite such a hungry mouth into a family that is already short of food?

PERSPECTIVE B:

THE SYSTEM IS FOR PROFIT AND THE NOT-FOR-PROFIT LABEL IS SIMPLY THE SUPERFICIAL APPEARANCE

The very fact that utilization rates can be pegged to reimbursement rates clearly demonstrates that the base motivation for medicine in Japan is profit. A critical and noteworthy example of the profit motive at work is the diagnosis and treatment of infections. Microbiology sensitivity testing is poorly reimbursed, and underutilized. By comparison, antibiotics are reimbursed relatively well, thus are overused.

Profit has been intrinsically designed into the system, mostly to the benefit of Japan Medical Association (JMA) members. Profit finds its way to JMA members through a complex set of 'tunnel' distribution companies. For example, if someone wants to do business at hospital X, they have to do business with dealer Y. It just so happens that dealer Y is the brother-in-law of the owner of hospital X. Even at the end of the day, if money is left over, physicians can simply pay themselves bonuses or take profit in other ways.

3. MARKET FORCES

There has been increased discussion about the role of market forces – and the range of responses has been extremely varied: from the very logical to the overly emotional. Although there seems little doubt that market forces will play an important role, to many this role needs to be minimized. To some, market forces seem the ideal way of forcing efficiencies into the system. But to others, market forces are merely a covert method for creating an unfair system that runs contrary to the interests of the less-wealthy classes.

Since the medical system's inception, the government has made great efforts to keep market forces at arm's length. First, it has created a different classification for medical corporations. It has also banned advertising, obsessively made all medical care non-profit, and has ensured that all treatments and products and physicians receive the exact same fees, regardless of experience or credentials.

For the past several years, opposition to market forces has lessened and new rules are being introduced that actually encourage them. Advertising is now permitted under certain circumstances. Hospitals are allowed to publicize things such as their accreditation status and the number of certified medical specialists on staff. Moreover, the new prospective payment type of reimbursement introduced into the university hospital system in Japan has an index that differentiates between hospitals' rates of reimbursement. It now appears that the market-forces camp is winning, albeit not without tremendous indignation from the JMA, politicians, and the socialist-minded general public.

PERSPECTIVE A:

DEMOGRAPHICS WILL FORCE MARKET DYNAMICS TO BECOME A REALITY

There is really no way that a country, such as Japan, with a heavily proportional elderly population can maintain a quality healthcare system purely using public funds. Faced with such a situation, it is inevitable that government will increasingly be forced to ration care to this elderly sector. The result will be a classic demand void and those who can afford it will seek alternatives such as privately funded healthcare facilities targeting the wealthier clientele. It should not be forgotten that the generation in question has the highest savings rate in the history of the modern world.

There are over 9,000 hospitals, 90,000 clinics and about 1.8 million hospital beds in Japan. As the government is forced to shorten hospital stays due to fiscal realities, these numbers will need to decrease dramatically. For example, if average hospital stays decrease to even double that of the average industrialized country, fully two-thirds of Japan's hospital beds will be unfilled. This reality clearly means that half the hospitals and clinics in Japan will need to close. The goal, therefore, should be for the best facilities to remain open while the worse are forced to close. How will this whittling down process occur unless through some kind of competition? And who will decide who wins this competition? Government bureaucrats? The only rational way to determine which hospitals survive is to make information available to patients and fee-payers so that they can choose where to receive care. These market forces will force hospitals to install quality systems, to compete, and to win – or otherwise be forced to close. The sad fact is that there are no longer enough excess funds to support the socialist ideals of the past.

PERSPECTIVE B:
WE MUST NOT ACCEPT MARKET DYNAMICS IN THE HEALTHCARE FIELD

If Japan is going to remain an egalitarian society in terms of healthcare delivery, classical market forces cannot be allowed to enter into the equation, particularly for the current graying population who have worked selflessly their whole lives for the betterment of Japan. To give preferential treatment to a business executive with money over, say, a factory worker, violates the social contract that has been Japan's conscience since the enactment of the current constitution. To selfishly allow an unfair distribution of healthcare will undermine the entire society.

Those who believe in these principles of fairness and equality understand the economic realities associated with maintaining a fair and equal system. In fact, Japan is not alone in this belief. Scandinavian countries such as Sweden and Denmark are excellent examples.

They have made the decision that high taxes are a small price to pay for fairness in society. What they get in return is a harmonious and relatively peaceful society. Do the Japanese really want to follow in the footsteps of the dog-eat-dog American model? Such ruthless competition is contrary to everything that Japan has built and is a great step backward. Yes, we will have to pay. Yes, there will be some lean times ahead due to demographics. But, it is a price that simply must be paid.

3 Political Perspectives

1. POLITICAL POWER IN JAPANESE HEALTHCARE

Since any discussion surrounding the politics of healthcare in Japan can be little more than superficial, it might be useful to simplify the discussion by paring it down to its base components. Three key groups are the major architects of healthcare policy development in Japan, namely:

1. Ministry of Health, Labour and Welfare (MHLW)
2. Japan Medical Association (JMA)
3. Ministry of Finance (MoF)

All these groups tend to be antagonistic towards one another, but the competitive nature of these relationships is best exemplified in the dynamic that exists with the MHLW and JMA as joint adversaries against the Ministry of Finance. The MoF derives its power from the fact that it controls the allocation and distribution of funds for all government programs. MoF bureaucrats have been eyeing healthcare with growing concern as it promises to suck up more and more public funds from the decreasing tax base indicative of an aging society. While the MoF frantically tries to stem the flow of funds to healthcare, the JMA is cautiously pressuring the MHLW to increase spending. The MHLW, spurred on by their strong socialistic leanings and intense pressure from the politically entrenched JMA, is fighting to at least maintain the status quo.

In this section on politics, we have left out what may be the most important factor – the general public. In the opinion of this author, however, the public currently has little say as to what policies the government actually implements. Unfortunate as it may be, at present the public is not really a political force at all.

PERSPECTIVE A:

THE POLITICAL SCENE REPRESENTS A HEALTHY BALANCE

No political system is perfect. Politics, by definition, depends on compromise between people or groups with conflicting ideas. Healthcare in Japan is no different. The MHLW is the main policy agency. They must build a coalition between the Japan Medical Association (JMA), and other professional groups such as the Japan Hospital Association, and even other governmental organizations such as the Ministry of Education (MoE). The final approval for rules affecting the spending of public funds comes from the Diet. The Diet hears arguments from the Ministry of Finance about the judicious utilization of funds and from the MHLW about public health needs. Of course there are also forces lobbying their case for each of the stakeholders. Of these, the most powerful lobby is the JMA.

Recently, the healthcare debate has seen increasing participation from both the medical industry and the general public. Before submitting anything to the Diet, the MHLW puts out nearly all significant proposed policy changes for public comment. They have also created an organization called the *Chuikyo* that serves as an advisory committee to the MHLW from industry and medical professional groups.

The bottom line is that healthcare in Japan is facing some major challenges. The political wheels are in place and they are working in the predictable fashion of any large government bureaucracy. Like any system, healthcare can be improved. The checks and balances are in place. There is ample opportunity for debate and discussion. And, in the end, decisions are made and rules enacted. This is a never-ending and necessary cycle that works.

PERSPECTIVE B:

THE POLITICAL SYSTEM IS BROKEN AND WILL RESULT IN DISASTER IF NOT FIXED

The main force influencing the political scene in relation to medicine in Japan is the Japan Medical Association (JMA). This group is composed primarily of private-sector physicians who own their own hospitals. They are politically well entrenched and have nearly unlimited financial resources, which means that the JMA controls the Diet through political contributions. Thus, the Diet makes sure that the MHLW does not diverge from the JMA's general policy goals. The only group capable of counterbalancing the JMA's political clout is the Ministry of Finance (MoF). While there have been some window-dressing attempts to involve the public, the average citizen's cries typically fall on deaf ears except when the system gets caught in scandal.

The JMA has been criticized for a number of reasons. First, that it is a power unto itself means it is almost a monopoly. Second, that the JMA's sole function is to maintain the status quo essentially defines the problems plaguing Japanese healthcare. The JMA resists change where change is needed and its goals are clearly member-oriented: to maintain members' preferential financial situation; and to make sure members are not inconvenienced with onerous regulations such as physician re-licensure requirements, meaningful hospital accreditation programs, or rules that take away from their stranglehold on patient medical information – something which helps stifle lawsuits and protects, once again, JMA members' financial fiefdoms.

The situation seems to be changing, however, since chinks are beginning to appear in the JMA's armor. The press and the public are openly criticizing the JMA and its policies. The government has been forced to support some programs calling for accountability in the medical profession – albeit most of these actions remain primarily voluntary in nature. Although there is a light at the end of the tunnel, in the end economic realities will dictate what happens.

2. PATIENT GROUPS

Patient advocacy is a relatively new development in healthcare in Japan. It began in the early 1990s with the HIV-tainted-blood scandal. This well-documented collaboration and collusion between the government and the private sector that ended in the infection of thousands of hemophiliacs with HIV marked the beginning of patient group activity in Japan. The survivors and their families banded together and have forced the government to accede to their positions successfully and repeatedly.

Since the HIV blood scandal, over a thousand patient groups have formed in Japan. These groups range from cancer survivors to those concerned with particular forms of certain diseases, cancer among them. Most of these groups are self-funded and many participate in the support of research for the disease of interest. They also act as support groups for their fellow sufferers and lobby the central government. The Internet has been a key form of communication and connectivity for these groups. Currently, most of these groups are poorly funded and not particularly well organized. In some cases, however, they are very vocal and outspoken on the issues important to them. Of late, the largest constituency of members comes from the swelling ranks of the elderly, who have the time and resources to dedicate to their cause.

With the noteworthy exception of hemophiliacs, patient groups have not – up to now – been a significant political force. While they may be becoming increasingly vocal, established political powers still control most of the decision-making. Based on actions and attitudes, it seems that patient groups appear to be nothing more than an annoyance to the current crop of healthcare power brokers. But, as the LDP's grip on the reins threatens to slip further, and these patient groups of older people begin to express their opinions at the ballot box, it is likely that their message may be increasingly heard.

PERSPECTIVE A:

PATIENT GROUPS ARE THE ONLY REAL ADVOCATES FOR QUALITY HEALTHCARE, AND THEIR VOICES SHOULD, AND WILL BE HEARD

Japanese politicians, bureaucrats, and the JMA have proven with their actions that they are unwilling or unable to act in the best interests of individual patients. Also, the issues of Japan's aging population and the country's overall economic problems have hijacked the agenda to the detriment of patients. The fundamental reason for this relegation of patient issues to the back burner is that the political power brokers do not consider patient care to be important enough. In fact, issues central to patient-centered care are essentially treated as secondary and trivial. For these reasons, it is imperative that patient groups have an increasingly louder voice in the healthcare debate.

Most patient groups are usually considered nothing more than a sometimes-noisy group of zealots with no significant funding or coordinated activities. As a result, those in power usually dismiss these groups out of hand. They are sometimes politely listened to, but usually are not taken seriously. If, in fact, we are looking for fair and balanced discussion and decision-making on healthcare issues, then we have to include a more patient-centric viewpoint in our discussions. If we do not, the process will remain incomplete.

The most obvious areas in which patient groups have legitimate concerns are technology adaptation and professional competency. Japan is notoriously slow in adopting new technologies, even when these technologies have proven to relieve symptoms or facilitate cures in other countries. While never admitted by those in power, the primary reason that these technologies are avoided is cost. Needless to say, no healthcare system can possibly supply all technologies to all patients regardless of cost. But, by ignoring patient input, there will always be a tendency to err on the side of saving money over patient benefit.

Professional competency is also an ongoing concern for patient groups. Even when proper technologies and medicines are adopted, without competent healthcare providers, efficacy can be limited and treatments can even become harmful. These concerns are particularly important in a system where doctors are licensed for life and there are no legal requirements for specialty physicians to take board examinations, nor are there any ongoing educational requirements.

The following steps need to be taken to ensure that the political balance becomes more equitable and patient-centric issues achieve more prominence:

1) Representatives from patient groups should be invited to join the MHLW Central Medical Committee (*Chuikyo*). They should be given a voice equal to those of physicians and industry members.
2) Representative from relevant patient groups should be invited to give opinions related to the approval and reimbursement of products associated with their diseases.
3) The MHLW should sponsor a website dedicated to individual patient groups. Information posted on this site should be monitored by MHLW and JMA members to help them understand issues important to patients.
4) Patient groups should band together and monitor politicians' voting records on healthcare issues. An awareness campaign should be undertaken at election time.
5) To fund themselves, patient groups should approach companies manufacturing or selling technologies related to their relevant diseases.
6) Medical information in Japanese should be made freely available to patients over the Internet about treatments available in Japan and elsewhere.

Patient views may well get in the way of the bold cost-saving measures which dominate the present healthcare agenda. Including these views, however, will supply much-needed balance. The views, opinions, and biases of patients need to be a significant part of the ongoing healthcare debate.

PERSPECTIVE B:

PATIENT GROUPS ARE REACTIONARY, UNINFORMED AND DO NOT UNDERSTAND THE CENTRAL ISSUES. HEALTHCARE POLICY SHOULD BE LEFT TO THE PROFESSIONALS

Being physically or mentally ill almost always creates extreme emotional or mental stress. This is especially true in cases where patients have a fatal, debilitating, or chronic condition. It is very easy to understand why individuals suffering from such afflictions want to associate with each other to discuss their conditions and for mutual consolation. It is also easy to understand how these patients, once organized, could turn their disease into a political cause, redirecting their anger and frustration about being sick towards hapless bureaucrats and politicians.

Current and future decisions surrounding healthcare in Japan are complex, technical, and sometimes political. The only way to make good and meaningful decisions is to limit the debate to rational and objective minds. To allow emotionally and physically charged individuals – who typically have little or no training in the areas they wish to participate – will lead only to more confusion and difficulties in the decision-making and implementation processes. While it is politically incorrect to say so, the reality is that there is no meaningful place for patient groups in political or governmental processes. These groups should be encouraged to act as support groups for members and are certainly encouraged to raise funds for research and other activities if they want to make a meaningful contribution.

3. THE MEDICAL INDUSTRY

The medical industry consists of several classes of companies. These include the giant pharmaceutical industry, the medical device and supply industry, the diagnostics industry, and the medical service industry. While these stakeholders are seldom mentioned in the current debate on healthcare reform in Japan, their roles are vital since they provide medical professionals with the tools they need to practice. Although we will examine all four of these industry segments independently, let us first take a look at the diverse perspectives relating to the appropriateness of industry participation in the debate at all.

PERSPECTIVE A:

THE MEDICAL INDUSTRY IS BIASED AND ONLY HAS PROFITS IN MIND. THEREFORE IT SHOULD NOT EVEN BE ALLOWED INTO THE HEALTHCARE DEBATE

The role of medical industries is clearly defined. Their first job is to meet the needs of medical professionals and develop products that practitioners need to best serve patients. Their other role is to help educate the medical profession about new technologies and to service those technologies as required. The incentive for these commercial entities is profit.

To allow profit-driven companies an active voice in the development of healthcare policy is to let the fox guard the henhouse. It is the job of medical industry executives to try and sell as many of their products as they can at prices as high as possible. They should not be faulted for this goal, however, since great value comes to medicine through the pursuit of self-interest. But to pretend that medical companies have the best interests of the healthcare system, the financial health of this system, or the overall well-being of patients is simply not supportable.

It is clear that the medical industry, with its nearly unlimited financial resources, is determined to influence the current debate on healthcare reform. It is also clear that they are willing to use political power and even threaten trade sanctions if left out of this debate. The government and the medical profession must do everything they can to ensure that these rich, powerful companies do not affect policy. Japanese healthcare policy needs to concern itself strictly with care delivery and be focused on the people dedicated to delivering it.

The medical industry has a role in healthcare – which should be limited to supplying and servicing products. The industry's current attempts to influence healthcare policy only serve to confuse and disrupt well-meaning professional groups, politicians, and bureaucrats, whose job is to create and implement policy.

PERSPECTIVE B:

THE FUTURE OF HEALTHCARE RELIES HEAVILY ON THE MEDICAL INDUSTRY'S INVESTMENT IN NEW TECHNOLOGIES AND IS A CRUCIAL COMPONENT IN THE HEALTHCARE DEBATE

Many of the gains in longevity, infant mortality, and overall health statistics often quoted in Japan are the direct result of medical technology. Increases in productivity in the delivery of healthcare in the future will also rely heavily on the development of new technologies. Since various medical industries are essential in developing these technologies, they are a key component of healthcare that cannot be ignored.

The argument that the medical industry should be excluded because they are profit driven simply does not make sense since this same logic would mean that doctors and private hospitals should be excluded as well. Just because there is a profit motive does not mean that a company (or doctor) does not want the system to improve. On the contrary, the ongoing success of the healthcare market relies on the success and value that the system and its technology bring to patients.

The medical industry is highly motivated to ensure that a rational system emerges from the current debate. It is also in a very good position to add value to the system. Since companies have experience in other health markets around the world, they have seen and dealt with many problems similar to those facing Japan and have seen what works and what does not. Excluding industry would be pointless and the waste of an excellent resource.

The last point about including the medical industry in the healthcare debate is one of balance. If physician groups and bureaucrats hold all the power in this debate, policies and funding will almost surely be unfairly and irrationally weighted towards doctors and hospitals. Such an imbalance could well create a system that ignores medical technology despite the successful role it has played in the healthcare system to date. New technology has been responsible for many of the advances in Japanese medicine and the medical industry should continue to contribute in the future as long as they are included as a meaningful partner in this debate. Including the medical industry will bring new perspectives and allow for more balanced policy decisions.

4 Legal Perspectives

1. MALPRACTICE

Until recently, medical malpractice suits were virtually unheard of in Japan. Since the public was only made aware of malpractice cases in the most egregious of circumstances, malpractice was therefore considered a rarity. Traditionally, the Japanese public has had great faith in its medical professionals and the medical system.

Even though doctors, hospitals, and insurance companies almost always choose to handle malpractice cases discretely and are eager to settle claims out of court, over the past decade the number of malpractice cases has increased dramatically and continues to rise. In spite of the growing number of cases, most experts contend that the quality of medical practice has not declined. Instead, these experts believe, the number of claims has risen due to other factors, such as: a) an increasing public demand for transparency; b) an increasing understanding that the system has intrinsic and indefensible faults; c) increased access to medical information; and d) willingness on the part of the legal profession to help patients pursue claims against medical practitioners.

Regardless of the reasons behind the growing number of malpractice claims, there is no question that this increase will continue and have a profound impact on medical care in Japan. Perhaps the most interesting aspect about medical malpractice in Japan when compared to the United States is that the financial incentives in Japan are relatively insignificant. In the US, successful plaintiffs can win millions of dollars even from malpractice that does not result in loss of life or disfigurement. In Japan, awards for even the worst cases of malpractice are peanuts in comparison. When combined with the fact that physicians and insurance companies are typically eager to settle out of court to avoid negative publicity, it is clear that malpractice in Japan is primarily a venue for venting anger against the medical system.

By and large, most Japanese people still consider resorting to legal measures to settle disputes as bad form and highly undesirable. Increasingly, however, there is a growing pro-litigation movement arising primarily from the desire to create a meaningful system of checks and balances where none exist now.

PERSPECTIVE A:

PEOPLE WHO RESORT TO MALPRACTICE SUITS ARE NOT TRULY JAPANESE

To err, as Alexander Pope said, is human. And since doctors are human, it stands to reason that they will make errors. A system that publicly humiliates or devastatingly punishes unintentional human error is nothing less than a dysfunctional system. Since malpractice suits clearly promote public demonization and can have a profound negative effect on a well-meaning doctor's career, they are dysfunctional too.

The practice of medicine is extremely complex and is as much art as science. Every single interaction between a physician and his patient is an amazingly complicated study of observation, decision-making, encyclopedic knowledge, psychology, action, and responsibility. The very thought that a physician must be held publicly accountable for some hindsight perception of wrongdoing made by some unaccountable observer after the fact is shameful and wrong. Malpractice suits, many people will tell you, seem more like money-grabbing opportunities by unscrupulous lawyers than real attempts to right some wrong.

Of course, it is understood that there is a need for checks and balances in the system, but the thing to understand is that there are already checks built into the system under the auspices of the various medical associations and through the traditional system of peer review. Suing for malpractice is an idea imported from the West and it is not suitable for Japan. In the West, a physician can shrug off a lawsuit and be practicing medicine again virtually the next day. Japanese society is unforgiving in such cases. The price of exposing the very few instances of legitimate malpractice that take place will only result in destroying the professional and personal lives of a great many good and honorable professionals. Perhaps the West needs this kind of punitive system. But, here, Japanese society already has a system for medical checks and balances that is demanding enough.

It is especially unfortunate that malpractice suits are increasing at a time when the healthcare system is experiencing other financial and structural stresses. The pressure that doctors will feel with someone looking over their shoulder and revisiting every decision they make will simply mean increased inefficiencies at a time when the system least needs them.

We need to do everything we can to limit the number of malpractice suits in Japan. We should encourage hospitals to offer patients proper venues so that they discuss any grievances clearly and directly with their physicians out of the public eye. As a society we need to understand that medical practitioners are not gods but people just like everyone else. We need to understand that sometimes mistakes are honest and unavoidable and should not be always punished. Finally, when true cases of malpractice arise, they should be handled not by the legal profession, but rather by relevant medical associations since they will have a much better idea about appropriate judgment and punishment.

Japan is already a harsh and unforgiving society. Western-style malpractice suits will only turn Japan into something nearly unbearable for well-meaning physicians and put even more financial pressure on an already overstressed system.

PERSPECTIVE B:

MEDICAL MALPRACTICE SUITS MAY BE ONE OF THE ONLY WAYS TO FORCE QUALITY AND TRANSPARENCY

From a young age, Japanese people are generally taught not to question authority. The teacher is *sensei*, a figure commanding respect and authority. High levels of respect have also traditionally been accorded government bureaucrats and banking officials and, until recently, their status has been essentially unquestioned. Unfortunately, this acceptance of perceived authority is the source of many of Japan's current problems and the average person feels the effects of this blind trust almost daily. The banks that we trusted with our money have mismanaged their portfolios into bankruptcy. The government officials responsible for our future are regularly seen being led off in handcuffs. And now we see the doctors whose instructions we followed unquestioningly exposed for incompetence and the human pain their incompetence has caused.

In many ways the medical profession is not solely to blame. Japanese society must also take some responsibility since we have neither challenged the medical profession nor demanded that it maintain the rigorous standards that a modern industrialized country deserves. Times, however, are changing. Just as we are now demanding higher standards of behavior from bankers and corporate executives through new legal initiatives, we must also do the same with the doctors, members of a profession that have become too used to operating beyond the reach of any measure of true accountability.

A rational and balanced system for dealing with malpractice would be extremely healthy for both the medical system and the medical profession since it would force physicians to keep up-to-date with new techniques and give them a financial incentive to adopt quality systems. It would also make them stop and think more carefully about every patient, knowing that they will be held accountable for their actions.

In spite of these statements it should be made clear that there are obvious detriments to allowing and expanding medical malpractice claims. Some individuals may attempt to enrich themselves at the expense of well-meaning physicians. There may also be a tendency for patients to have unrealistic expectations of their doctors – especially when emotionally stressed after some heart-wrenching health drama. We also run the risk of increasing the burden on hospitals and medical professionals if they are constantly forced to defend themselves legally.

Despite all the negatives, however, it is impossible to ignore an option that – even if flawed – goes some way to correcting a broken system in which doctors hold all of the power and only patients suffer the consequences. Physicians, like everyone, need to be challenged in order to excel and the current system is wholly unequipped to offer any meaningful challenges or checks. The threat of lawsuit is a both a warning and a motivation for both hospitals and a physicians to treat each and every case with their full attention. This threat is also a guarantee that the systems and qualifications that are so central to top-quality medical care are as good as they can be. And, for those who trespass against the weak and infirm, lawsuits punish the wrongdoers where they are most vulnerable – in their wallets.

The government should adopt measures that give legal relief to patients who have been harmed through inadequate or incompetent care. One option is to create a branch of the legal profession dedicated to prosecuting these kinds of cases. We could also open hotlines where patients can report malpractice directly to the MHLW. Physicians should also be appointed as judges so that medical malpractice cases can be fully understood by the courts. Lastly, and to ensure that fairness and equality is preserved and frivolous or malicious cases prevented, there should be significant and meaningful punishments for those who make and pursue false malpractice claims.

2. INFORMED CONSENT

In healthcare terms, informed consent is when patients are made aware of the risks and benefits of treatment or other medical procedures. In Western countries, the transition from the 'doctor-knows-best' style of medical practice to an informed-consent style of practice took place in the 1970s–80s. This transformation was brought about by a number of factors, not the least of which was the increase in malpractice litigation. What informed consent now means in the West is that patients become part of, and more responsible for, the decision-making process for their own treatment.

In Japan informed consent, while discussed and debated on an intellectual level, has not seem any real practical application. The only possible exception is in the area of clinical trials, where the new Good Clinical Practice (GCP) guidelines specify that doctors must inform their patients when they will be exposed to an unapproved treatment so that they can understand the risks (and/or benefits) associated with the treatment. To demonstrate the depth of professional aversion to informed consent, the adoption of GCP guidelines has drastically slowed the development of clinical trials in Japan.

PERSPECTIVE A:

INFORMED CONSENT IS A POOR FIT FOR JAPANESE CULTURE AND SENSIBILITIES

There is a trend in Japan these days that overrates Western ideas and values and underrates Japanese ones. There is a great danger to this trend since traditional Japanese values and sensibilities, developed with wisdom and sensitivity over centuries, may fall prey to this Western flavor of the week, a kind of fear of liability that is often disguised under the noble heading of 'logic.' Of course, there is a certain' logic' to informing patients of available treatment types. Of course there is a certain logic' to discussing with patients statistically relevant prognoses relating to one treatment vs. another. As soon as one goes face to face with a critically ill patient, parent, or loved one, however, this kind of 'logic' is nothing more than cruel and cold and a denial of other traditional values like compassion, understanding, and empathy.

All cultures have some patients who want or even need to be involved in their treatment decisions. There are also patients that prefer to have their physicians make decisions on their behalf. Surely it is up to the judgment of every doctor to try and decide what kind of patient and what kind of situation the patient is in and, based on this assessment, make a decision about informed consent. Of course, situations like this lead to debates about doctors playing God and the potential disaster that can result when humans try and rise above their station. Naturally, some doctors are very good at understanding the needs of their patients. Others may misunderstand. But, in the doctors' defense, most physicians deal with these kinds of situations many times a day. They are practiced at learning to understand circumstances, particularly in regard to patients' intrinsic needs. They also understand the science of the medicine they prescribe and, very importantly, they gain the kind of insight that only seeing thousands of patients can provide. Compare this knowledge and objective experience with that of a patient who is probably both physically ill and emotionally distraught. Moreover, can untrained laymen understand and assess the complexities of the medical science related to their treatment? In many cases, it is clear, patients themselves are in the absolutely worst position possible to make sound, objective judgments about the most correct therapeutic course.

There are also practical issues to be dealt with. In traditional Japanese medicine practices, physicians determine diagnosis and treatment and do not typically ask the opinion of the patient. Alternatively, the Western approach is to try and explain the complexities of the science and outline the statistical analysis of the various options. What Western doctors are doing, it could be argued, is essentially wasting valuable time and resourses to try and explain the issues to patients who then have the responsibility of making a critical decision without the benefit of a doctor's training, knowledge, and experience. With most cases, is not this kind of medical practice, wasteful, and inefficient? And could not it well be the cause of poor – even dangerous – clinical decision-making?

Of course, there is a time and a place for informed consent. But as to when and where – that should be the doctor's decision. Using informed consent to minimize malpractice liability is not only poor clinical practice, it is also wasteful and a denial of a doctor's ethical responsibilities.

PERSPECTIVE B:

INFORMED CONSENT IS A NATURAL PART OF A MATURE HEALTHCARE SYSTEM

From a historical context, the notion of informed consent is a relatively new one. Despite its relative newness, however, in most Western countries informed consent has become the accepted status quo. Japan, however, is the exception, which is perhaps not surprising when considering the history of Japan's medical system and how it underwent an almost total reincarnation in the early 1950s. In contrast, at the same time that the Japanese healthcare model was being reborn, the American medical establishment was already well on the path towards what we now call modern medicine.

To many outside observers, the lack of an ingrained informed consent system in Japan is disconcerting. From the standpoint of Western contemporary mores, such an absence violates the basic right of individuals to make decisions about their own health – arguably the most important thing in any person's life. A lack of informed consent also transforms physicians into demi-gods, ones who hold the very lives of the patients in their hands, even though their skill and knowledge levels vary from the very high to the very low and un-godlike, indeed.

The most troubling part surrounding the lack of informed consent in Japan is the highly questionable training and licensing requirements – or lack thereof – for Japanese physicians. There is a lack of meaningful residency programs. A lack of requisite ongoing medical education. Licensing is for life. Compounding these training and education issues is the absence of meaningful checks and balances in the form of hospital accreditation programs or the threat of malpractice suits. Knowing this, how would you feel about totally entrusting your diagnostic and treatment decisions – your life – to this system or these physicians?

Japan is, however, inexorably moving towards informed consent. Passing laws and creating rules is the easy part of building this system. The difficult part is changing the culture of Japanese medical associations and the attitudes of patients. For meaningful informed consent to occur, the following things must happen:

1) Patients will need the capacity to launch meaningful malpractice suits against doctors and hospitals. In tandem, a legal specialty needs to be created specifically for medical malpractice. The dual threat/incentive nature of malpractice litigation will force the system to inform the patient.
2) Physicians will need to receive better training on an ongoing basis. No doctor will willingly promote informed consent if it threatens to expose him or her as ignorant.
3) Patient medical information needs to be made more available to patients. Information on patient charts should belong to the patient – not the physician. More health information should be made available in Japanese over the Internet.

In summary, the creation of an informed consent system is an evolutionary process and will occur in Japan over time. For a system of informed consent to occur, however, structural changes to the current system must happen. These changes include the development of an adequate medical malpractice system so that physicians can be held more accountable and patients have more recourse. Stricter educational and licensing requirements for physicians are two other necessary changes that must be made.

3. PATIENT RECORDS

Under current Japanese law, patient records are the property of the physician or hospital. Patients or patients' families have no right to the information in his or her medical record. The only legal way that a hospital can be forced to reveal a patient's file is through court order.

In response to the public outcry about access to patient records, the government has recently taken several steps. The JMA has claimed that it is a financial and functional burden for hospitals to make patient chart information available so the government has agreed to pay a small reimbursement to hospitals that do so voluntarily. Hospitals can also charge patients a reasonable fee to make copies of relevant information. As well, it has been mandated that all national hospitals make patient information available on request with the appropriate payment of fees. In response to these initiatives, a number of private hospitals have also created policies opening chart information to patients.

While many people may feel that the long battle over patient charts was a plot to hide medical errors, it was really only a tactical business decision. If patients have copies of their chart, it is very simple for them to move to other hospitals for treatment. If however, hospitals maintain ownership of charts, it makes it cumbersome for patients to go elsewhere – especially those who are experiencing chronic diseases with ongoing treatment requirements. These are the patients that tend to be cash cows for hospitals and clinics.

A push is currently underway to store patient records electronically. Insiders fear that such storage could one day make it possible for patients to go to any hospital since records would be available anywhere at any time. Opponents point to privacy concerns with such a system. In response, it has been suggested that patients themselves could keep their own data in an electronic format that can be read and updated by any hospital they visit. This system, it is argued, would allow patients more freedom to move from facility to facility and would save money by not having to repeat tests and procedures. An electronic patient record system could also decrease over-medication and other medical errors.

The importance of this seemingly minor issue should not be underestimated. Opening patient charts would increase patient choice, reduce errors, and expose them more readily when they do occur. It could even ultimately help promote a system for collecting meaningful data on patient outcomes and doctor and hospital performance. On the negative side, there is a real issue with patient privacy, a problem that will likely stifle progress for the time being. The debate rages on.

PERSPECTIVE A:

OPENING PATIENT CHART INFORMATION COULD BE DETRIMENTAL TO PATIENTS, TO HOSPITALS, AND TO THE OVERALL COST OF ADMINISTERING HEALTHCARE

In theory, the idea sounds wonderful. Provide greater access to patient charts, goes the argument, and patients can participate more fully in their healthcare. Put this information in a database, promoters of this idea contend, so that statistically relevant data can be accrued, analyzed, and used to monitor the performance of hospitals and physicians. Before we look at the theory, however, let us face the realities. First, opening patient charts could have an overtly negative effect on patient care in some cases. Second, such a step will create a bureaucratic nightmare and could eventually drive good medical professionals away from the field.

As with everything related to healthcare, the paramount concern must be patient care. In some cases, it may be beneficial for patients to have access to their chart information. In other cases, patients may not be emotionally, psychologically, or intellectually able to cope with the burden of knowing every single detail about their case. The only person who can provide answers about a patient's ability to deal with this kind of situation is, of course, the patient's primary-care physician. The decision about whether or not to open this information is not based on secrecy or paranoia. Instead it is to protect patients who may actually be hurt by what they find when every piece of information, large or small, sees the light of day.

Opening information will also have a negative impact on the overall efficiency of the healthcare system. Some patients may have the tendency to burden their doctors with unreasonable requests for information. They may also jump from one facility to another until they get an answer they want to hear. There may also be an increase in the number of frivolous lawsuits from emotionally-stressed patients or families.

If an electronic format is used to increase the transparency of patient data, the aforementioned problems will be increased exponentially. Physicians will become almost secretive about what they put on a chart rather than be focused on the patient. It will create a paranoid system where doctors can be ranked and judged for whatever they entered in a chart years before. If this grand scheme envisioned by some actually occurs, it could well drive out some of the profession's best talent. Could you take someone constantly second-guessing your decisions and trying to force you to practice medicine by formula instead of your own clinical judgment?

It is important to realize that the practice of medicine is as much art as science. Patients, of course, prefer to view medicine as a science. But, if patients' charts are opened and patients parade them before other physicians there will be always be a difference of opinion and judgment. While such differences are both natural and healthy, they are also a reflection of the imperfect nature of medical practice. Such imperfection may confuse and even anger patients who, up to now, thought of their doctors as infallible. As a result, patients may postpone therapy until they get some kind of definitive answer – which may well work against them by delaying needed treatment. Such a situation will frustrate everyone in the system.

Finally, while some may claim that there are technical ways to protect electronic data, as you will know from the media, successful hacks are made into even the best-protected systems almost daily. The system envisioned by promoters of the open information plan would be accessible from thousands of sites and by tens of thousands of people. Insurance companies, employers, and even prospective suitors will want this information. Regardless of how secure a system is, it will never be better than a paper file locked away in a doctor's office.

The decision to open a patient's file or not should be the physician's alone. To legislate the opening of records will add another layer of bureaucracy as well as potentially decreasing overall levels of patient care. Creating a digital database of patient records will promote a Big Brother environment where everyone will be looking constantly over their shoulders. Such a step could well drive away good medical practitioners and decrease the efficiency of the system as a whole.

PERSPECTIVE B:

MAKING PATIENT CHART INFORMATION READILY AVAILABLE IS THE KEY TO CREATING TRANSPARENCY, ACCOUNTABILITY, AND TO INCREASING EFFICIENCY. THERE ARE TECHNICAL SOLUTIONS TO THE PRIVACY ISSUES

The information contained in a patient chart belongs solely to that patient or – in some circumstances – to his or her family. The idea that one person owns another person's medical records is a throwback to a time when physicians were considered gods, a notion that is insulting in a progressive society. Above and beyond the ethical issues concerning who 'owns' somebody's health information, the greater availability of information will also have many other advantages.

If doctors or hospitals know that patient records can be taken to another hospital by a patient and that other physicians may look at them, the incentive to keep good records and to use the latest treatments becomes greater for the original care providers. Doctors who fail to meet their professional commitments will become known to their colleagues, and ultimately by a professional review committee for corrective action. In cases of gross malpractice, a newer open system would give patients the ammunition they need to address grievances.

Figure 17. Malpractice litigations in Japan

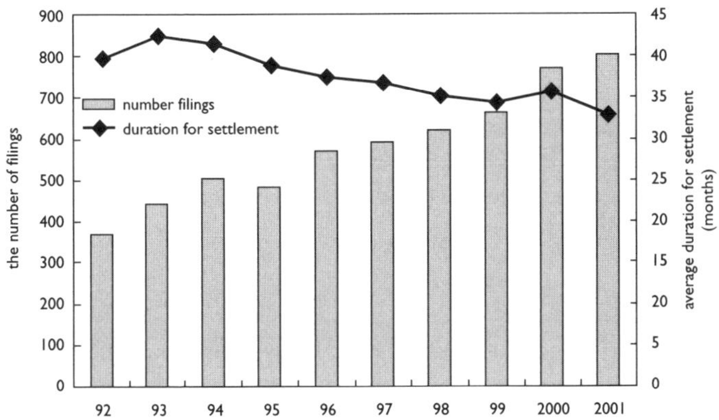

Source: Supreme Court

While the ability to motivate physicians and expose incompetence in the medical profession is a definite argument for opening patient records, it is nothing compared to the advantages of storing records electronically. By storing data digitally, a patient's total chart information becomes accessible to the hospital's entire team of medical professionals. Such a system would mean better and more communication, thus decreasing errors and increasing efficiencies. If data access is widened to include a centralized database, medical professionals will be better able to track different diseases and treatments and then identify best practices with statistically relevant outcomes.

There is no question that patient privacy is a very real and important issue. But, it is also overused as an excuse by physicians for keeping records closed. Instead, one suspects, what really concerns doctors is holding on to their patients and keeping potential problems secret. There are technical ways to keep this kind of data secure and private. That security measures that are routinely used in the financial sector can surely be modified and used for medical records. Ideas for keeping information private include having patients maintain physical possession of their own PIN that would be needed for accessing the central database. Another suggestion is for the data to be stored on data strips or cards to be kept by the patient. For centralized data used in outcome studies, patient identities can be deleted prior to uploading. Yes, privacy is an issue, but it should not be an impediment to implementing electronic patient charts.

A patient's chart should be made available to that patient whenever they ask. In fact, access to this information should be a right granted by law. Doing so will give patients the freedom to change hospitals and will help remove the secrecy that exists now and protects incompetent medical practices. Such a step will also encourage doctors to learn new methods and stay on top of their field. Patient privacy issues need to be seen as a problem to overcome, not as the end of the discussion.

4. INDUSTRY SALES AND PROMOTION CODES

In the past, the relationship between doctors and companies wanting to sell products into the medical market was very close indeed. Physicians learned to expect substantial favors from these industry relationships such as trips, lavish entertainment, or free samples that could be resold for good profit. All of these perks were commonplace until recently.

In the year 2001, medical companies implemented a voluntary code of ethics that has greatly curtailed these benefits for Japanese doctors. While this code does have some built-in flexibility, it has virtually eliminated – for fear of jail – lavish entertainment and has greatly decreased the amount of samples a representative can give to a physician. It has also limited to one year (from a product's launch date) the time in which samples can be given. Thereafter, no further samples can be given.

These steps are backed up by the government's code relating to the promotion of products at government-funded facilities. This code essentially stopped any and all perks. Medical reps cannot even buy a government doctor a cup of coffee.

The government has also proclaimed that medical reps can only provide information specific to their own products and may not supply other peripheral information. At this same time, the pharmaceutical industry has voluntarily mandated a strict testing system that all medical representatives must pass so that they are permitted to call on doctors. They also have minimum ongoing training requirements. The goal is to use this army of 50,000 medical representatives to engage and educate physicians on the proper use of their products.

PERSPECTIVE A:

THE NEW PROMOTION RULES ARE FOOLISH AND ILL-ADVISED

While it is clearly understood that there were abuses in the past regarding favors for physicians by company reps, it is equally clear that the new rules have done more harm than good. What they have done is remove all incentives for doctors to make time for medical representatives. In the past, medical reps could count on long periods of discussion while entertaining. Doctors would, in turn, yield time from their busy schedules to listen to these representatives. Doctors knew that some of the information provided was propaganda and some hard data, but for the most part, they knew how to sort out the information wheat from the chaff.

The fact is that doctors are very busy people. They are also human. While they want to study and learn more about ever-changing medical technologies, reality makes it difficult to find time to do so. The favors given to physicians by medical sales reps provided the incentive and the environment for meaningful dialogue. The relationships that were developed between these reps and their doctor clients also served other important functions. For example, it was easy for a doctor to pick up the phone and ask questions about new treatments and to help locate comparison data. Now, technically, it is not even legal for a company rep to buy a government-paid doctor a cup of coffee – let alone help him with his research.

Most doctors are not well paid, particularly in comparison with their Western counterparts. This low-level pay is a reality than cannot be ignored. The fact is, that for many of these physicians, the favors provided by the company representative were an important part of their compensation for being a doctor. It allowed them time to go out and relieve stress. The rep-doctor relationship sometimes even helped them augment their meager incomes through the sale of sample products. While the government is quick to take these things away, who will replace this part of a physician's income?

While it is understood that the rules have been made, and that there is no going back, the medical industry and physicians alike should be encouraged to find loopholes in these rules in order to keep the important and valuable relationship between doctors and company reps intact. Failing to do so may decrease the overall knowledge of the medical profession, decrease job satisfaction, and – most importantly – lower the level of patient care.

PERSPECTIVE B:

USING SKILLED MEDICAL REPRESENTATIVES MORE EFFECTIVELY IS A GOOD GOAL AND SHOULD BE PURSUED

It is about time the relationship between medical company representatives and physicians was scrutinized. Let us be brutally frank about things because this is how they worked: if a company rep wined and dined a physician enough; if he was at the beck-and-call of the doctor at all hours; if special favors were granted that ranged from women to golf outings; if a rep did all of this in enough quantity for a long enough period of time then the doctor would prescribe the rep's product to his patients. Some may dispute this reality, or call it overstated. Insiders, however, recognize the scenario all too well and know it to be true.

The reality is that the kinds of practices described above have resulted in patients being given inappropriate drugs. These practices have resulted in patients being given drugs that they do not need. The behavior described above has resulted in increased spending on medical products – especially pharmaceuticals. Not only has this kind of behavior resulted in an increase in the volume of the sales of products, the practice has also resulted in higher prices. The 50,000 sales representatives and their lavish entertainment expense accounts cost money. Ultimately this cost gets passed on to the consumer.

The new rules limiting what favors medical reps can provide for doctors are outstanding and come none too soon. It is interesting that representatives are now complaining that physicians will not make time for them now that they cannot provide favors. Is not that the clearest indicator that the real, medical value of sales reps was limited and possibly even negligible?

> We should all applaud the MHLW`s requirement that all medical reps be trained and tested on an ongoing basis in the hope for a 'trickle-down' effect to doctors. But would not it be even better if we had new rules saying that physicians require ongoing education and testing instead? Would not it be much more effective for everyone if the billions of dollars that medical companies spend on sales promotions went to funding quality and accountable education instead?

5. INDUSTRY REGULATIONS

Regulations surrounding the approval, importation, and sale of medical products will always be complex. While the rules are in place ostensibly to ensure the safety and efficacy of medical products, it is also an ideal way for the government to achieve some slightly more clandestine goals. These regulations, for example, can be used to favor domestically-manufactured products over imports as well as to protect the interests of certain stakeholders – such as domestic importers and dealers.

In the case of medical devices, there are four categories of products. Class I products are referred to as general medical products; these are low risk and typically are substantially equivalent to other existing products. Class II goods are considered controlled medical products while Class III and IV-type products are categorized as higher risk. Changes due to take effect in April 2004 state that importers who deal in Class III and IV products will be required to employ certain kinds of staff: a safety manager, a quality assurance manager, and an auditor. This may significantly increase the regulatory burden for many medical companies operating in Japan.

Another big change, this time due to go into effect in April 2005, is the elimination of in-country caretakers. This uniquely Japanese system, which began in the late 1980s and developed into a cottage industry, was created to allow foreign manufacturers without a physical presence in Japan to gain and maintain product approvals. The MHLW has decided, however, that this practice has got out of hand and will abandon it. The new law will mean that many small firms will be unable to do business without going through large companies already in the field. It may also drive some companies completely out of the market.

The regulatory approval process has another basic function besides satisfying safety and efficacy concerns. It also acts as the gatekeeper for establishing reimbursement rates. This final regulatory step before a product is allowed to go to market is key for manufacturers attempting to succeed in Japan. It is also an important way in which the government tries to control costs.

PERSPECTIVE A:

RECENT REGULATORY CHANGES HAVE BEEN PUT INTO PLACE TO PROTECT LOCAL MANUFACTURERS AND DEALERS AND TO KEEP NEW TECHNOLOGIES FROM REACHING THE MARKET. PATIENTS WILL BE THE BIGGEST LOSERS

The net effect of new industry regulations is to increase the number of employees that companies need to fulfill their regulatory requirements. These rules will also limit the ability to outsource regulatory-related work to subcontractors. Finally, the new restrictions will also protect the position of medical product dealers. Because the new regulations address none of the system's underlying problems, however, these new rules will not achieve their stated goal of making Japanese medical care safer.

If the goal of the new rules is to limit and slow the entry of new medical technologies into Japan, they should be a great success. Large companies will most certainly look very carefully at this new situation since regulatory expenses are very high and the chances of gaining a good reimbursement rate are very low. Small firms which previously relied on the successful in-country caretaker system will need to return to business relationships with the trading companies that they previously worked so hard to escape.

If the MHLW really wants to improve the safety of medical products, it should start by looking inside its own walls. The people that review regulatory applications simply do not have the necessary expertise to understand everything that passes over their desks and the nonsensical questions coming back from the ministry to industry people are infamous. Perhaps even worse, there are not enough reviewers to handle current application levels and the review department backlog is unjustifiable. The MHLW should also look at the healthcare providers who use these products and ensure that they use them efficiently and appropriately. Besides being unfair, placing all of the regulatory burden on medical manufacturers and importers simply increases costs in an attempt to make things look like they are improving. True change needs to come from two places: from the government bureaucrats and at the point of patient care. It is simply too easy to mandate stricter regulations at the expense of the medical industry – which is, incidentally, the only stakeholder in the debate devoid of political clout.

PERSPECTIVE B:

RECENT REGULATORY CHANGES ARE RATIONAL AND MAKE THE SYSTEM MORE TRANSPARENT AND SAFER. THEY WILL ALSO HELP CONTROL SPENDING BY DECREASING THE APPROVAL OF PRODUCTS THAT DO NOT HAVE CLEAR EFFICACY

The state of regulatory affairs for medical products in Japan has been, and remains, poor. Sub-standard work in the area of regulatory approvals has seen many ineffective products approved. In some cases, patients have even been put at risk because of the approval of dangerous products. Product recalls, too, have been nearly impossible to manage. There are also myriad – and possibly unsolvable problems connected to accountability and other areas relating to the import and sale of products.

Let us look at the regulations. First of all, as a manufacturer or importer you would need to employ an appropriately-trained quality assurance officer. This person's job is to ensure that your products have been appropriately tested and are free of defects. You will also need a safety officer. This employee's responsibility is to ensure that patient safety concerns are addressed during things like product recalls. Finally, you will need an independent regulatory auditor whose responsibility is to oversee the entire process and take responsibility for its integrity. What is so onerous about these safety-oriented requirements?

Changes were made to the in-country-caretaker system because it was rife with problems. This system allowed small and large companies alike to use middlemen to perform regulatory functions on their behalf. It also allowed companies to pass the culpability for poor regulatory practices onto a third party. While there are certainly qualified and diligent in-country caretakers, there are also a great many fly-by-night operations that perform this kind of work for low prices and with low quality. It is about time that this system was abolished since it was jeopardizing the integrity of the entire regulatory system.

Now that these necessary changes have been agreed to, it is time for the government to begin looking inwards and employ more qualified staff as reviewers. The government must also take steps to change how it uses the regulatory process; this should not be a system for restricting certain medical technologies from the Japanese market. Lastly, once a product is approved for use, an appropriate reimbursement rate needs to be set relative to the value it brings to patients.

The new regulatory rules are fair and equitable. They need augmenting by more qualified reviewers, however. The system should not be used to block the introduction of new technologies or negatively affect the reimbursement of these technologies.

5 Area-specific Points of Debate

1. HOME HEALTHCARE

The Japanese government has made it a national priority to provide home healthcare services to its aged population. The thinking behind this plan is that keeping the elderly at home and out of the hospital longer through home-care services will help lessen the burden on the healthcare system. To this end, the government has sanctioned something called the '*kaigo*' system whereby limited reimbursement is offered to private companies that provide home healthcare services to the qualified elderly.

PERSPECTIVE A: THE *KAIGO* SYSTEM IS BENEFICIAL

One must consider several factors when looking at the home healthcare programs adopted by the government in 2002. The first factor is that, as society ages, our elderly will need help. Although this help could occur in hospitals, the result would be higher costs and care would be less humane because it would involve taking the elderly from their homes. The other factor is that the faltering economy has created the worst employment situation since the war. Moreover, unemployment is worst among young women.

The *kaigo* system requires a large number of home helpers and could effectively take many people – primarily women – off the unemployment lines and turn them into productive tax-paying citizens. This is a win-win situation: we help the elderly stay in their homes longer and lessen the financial and structural burden on the healthcare system.

Critics say that the government-sponsored funding is simply not enough to create an economically viable business for *kaigo* home helpers. The answer to these people is that the government is merely priming the pump with limited funds that can be augmented by the private sector later. The law specific to the *kaigo* system should not be forgotten since it allows and promotes mixed private and public insurance and other payments (*kongyo shingyo*). This flexible approach means that elderly people with the funds to do so can augment payment and receive increased services. It also allows the younger segments of the population to plan for the future by purchasing *kaigo* insurance which provides a boost to the insurance industry and the overall economy.

The government should be praised for introducing this program. It should be supported financially and even expanded to include non-elderly disabled citizens.

Figure 18. Trend in the number of people with disabilities

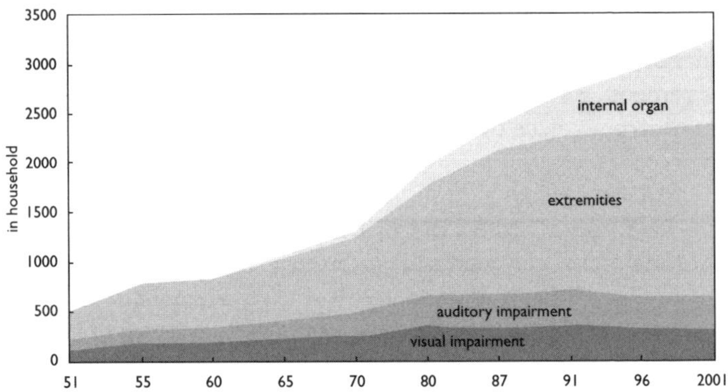

Source: 'Public Health of Japan 2002,' Japan Public Health Association

PERSPECTIVE B:

THE *KAIGO* SYSTEM CONCOCTED BY THE GOVERNMENT IS COSTLY AND INEFFECTIVE

Of course older people want to stay in their homes as long as possible. Spending your final years in a hospital is not a pleasant thought for any of us. But, the home helper system as it is currently implemented is ill-conceived, costly, and offers little or no value to the citizens it is designed to help.

The first problem is that the proposed reimbursement is too low. It will not be economically feasible for individuals or companies to make a profit. A home visit will be reimbursed at a rate of only ¥700. For this, home helpers need to travel to the site which takes time and train-fare. Even if the helper spends only thirty minutes with their client, her or his highest possible wage will be around ¥500 per hour – excluding the cost of any equipment or other expenses. By comparison, the lowest wage in fast food restaurants is ¥800/hour.

Figure 19. Salaries of long-term care staff

(Unit yen)

Monthly salary by occupation		Salary by type of payment		Salary by type of employment	
1st class helper	190,018	Full-time employee (monthly salary)	226,677	Monthly pay	224,726
2nd class helper	130,736	Full-time employee (hourly salary)	1,021	Daily pay	8,183
3rd class helper	116,434	Short-time employee (hourly salary)	1,022	Hourly pay	1,203
Care manager	276,057	Part-time employee (hourly salary)	1,329		

Source: Care Worker Support Center Foundation, 'Investigating on Long-Term Care at Offices (2001)'

Although clients can augment this fee to make it more economically viable, as a business, most companies simply cheat. As a rule, the elderly do not make complaints and are easily confused. The result is that unscrupulous companies make a profit by lowering their staff and service standards.

The next problem with the *kaigo* system is the lack of quality training received by the care-givers. As mentioned, the low reimbursement rates necessitate a low-cost labor force and, accordingly, these workers are generally untrained and undereducated for their professional tasks. The system, therefore, has been structured so that poorly educated, poorly trained people from lower economic classes will visit the homes of vulnerable elderly people – many living alone and many in ill health. If this is not a recipe for disaster, then it is hard to see what is: the potential for theft, abuse and – at the very least – substandard care is frightening.

A final point worth making concerns the economics of caring for people in their homes. A single well-trained nurse can care for up to twenty patients an hour in a predictable manner with highly professional standards. This nurse is also backed up by full dietary, pharmacy, physical therapy, and physician services when the need arises. In the case of home care, this same nurse (assuming she or he would be willing to work for ¥500/hour) would be able to interface with only one or two patients during the same one-hour period. The fundamental economics of the kaigo system simply do not work.

The *kaigo* home-care system should either be scrapped or done properly. To make it work, the following things should be done:

a) increase the reimbursement to make it economically feasible;
b) have mandatory training, testing, and certification for all home helpers;
c) create a certification system for companies employing home helpers; and
d) implement a system of checks to ensure that the elderly are not abused and become victims of a system designed to help them.

2. EMERGENCY MEDICINE

The shortfalls of Japanese medical care are nowhere more glaring than in the area of emergency medicine. Most healthcare observers and even insiders readily admit that emergency medicine in Japan is far behind that of other industrialized nations. One reason for this gap are the regulations which greatly limit what Emergency Medical Technicians (EMTs) can do in crisis situations since physicians can only legally perform even the most basic treatments. It is noteworthy that, although there have recently been training courses set up for EMTs to learn more invasive therapies, these newly-learned skills will not be practically applicable until the laws limiting their activities are changed. It is generally believed that these factors, together with low reimbursement rates for emergency treatments, are major factors behind Japan's less than stellar reputation in the area of emergency medicine.

Some observers suggest this is an area of Japanese medicine that needs a thorough overhaul while others have a different perspective.

PERSPECTIVE A:

EMERGENCY MEDICINE IS A QUESTION OF PRIORITIES

There is no question that emergency medicine in Japan falls short of that available in, say, the United States. But, the fact is that quality emergency medicine is very expensive and has relatively low success rates. With funds for medical care growing increasingly tight, should

Japan really spend huge sums of money on the high-tech ambulances, helicopters, field treatment materials, and hugely expensive trauma centers in regional hospitals that are needed to have a more effective emergency medicine program?

Of course Japanese people cherish life and want to avoid preventable death as much as anyone anywhere. That is not the point. Instead, the point is that policy-makers are faced with competing priorities and they have taken the hard and not necessarily popular decisions necessary to achieve a balance between the medical needs of the average person and those of people needing expensive emergency care.

Being realistic, emergencies are a kind of fate that await us all. Can the government be held responsible for the unavoidable destinies of the very few at the expense of the many? Of course, this kind of choice is a moral dilemma – but it is one to which rational thinking must be applied. Given the limited resources available, it is simply more effective to spend our limited funds on manageable diseases with a high success rate, rather that on hugely expensive treatments for a luckless few.

PERSPECTIVE B:

A MODERN SOCIETY DESERVES QUALITY EMERGENCY MEDICINE

The problem with emergency medicine in Japan is not a lack of funds. Rather, the poor state we are in is a direct result of the egoists who stonewall sensible policy decisions; in other words, the physician lobby. The reason that even the most basic of emergency care procedures can only be done by doctors is not because of money issues – it is purely because of the physician lobby. Even the standard first-aid procedures that are taught to elementary school students in some industrialized countries are forbidden to be performed by anyone but doctors in Japan. When Emergency Medical Technicians (EMTs) arrive on the scene, they simply put the patient on the stretcher and then into the ambulance. There is no attempt to resuscitate victims, stop bleeding, or to do any other triage procedures that would seem absolutely vital. To compound things, when victims finally arrive at the hospital, there will most likely be no board-certified emergency physicians available. At night, for example, unlucky victims will likely get a young intern lacking the experience or know-how to treat badly-injured patients.

Admittedly, Japan needs to invest more in some of the latest emergency equipment both for the field and hospital emergency rooms. But, more than financial investment, we need to invest in new laws concerning personnel eligible to treat emergent patients. We need to invest in the education of our medical professionals about how to treat emergency patients. And, most of all, we need to introduce basic first-aid training into the public school system so that everyone understands the basics. More than anything, educating the young and the public will change the behavior and attitude of the population that fate is not an unwinnable lottery and that we can help victims of emergencies through knowledge and action.

To repeat: this problem is not about money. It is about the JMA refusing to support specialty education for emergency-room physicians and about government bureaucrats unwilling to stand up to these physician groups and create rational rules backed up with proper information and training.

3. CANCER AND CHEMOTHERAPY

There are some noteworthy differences in how cancer is treated in Japan vs. how it is done in the United States. While this is not the venue to make clinical judgments about one method being better than another, we can point out that there is a strong bias in Japan against high-dose chemotherapy in favor of lower-dose treatments. Again, there are a number of perspectives as to why this is.

Figure 20. Cancer mortality (female)

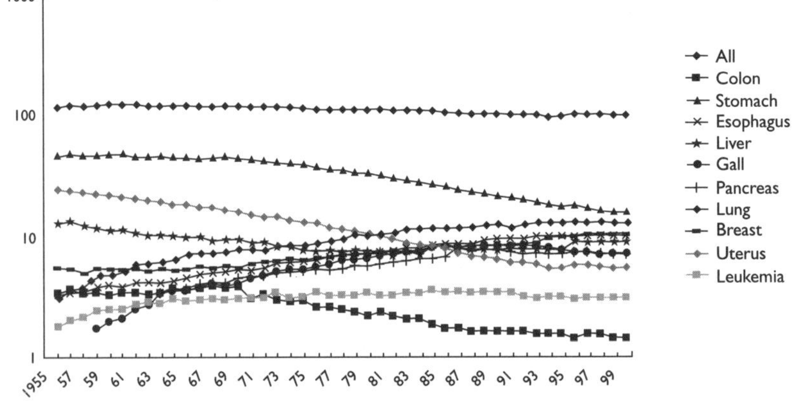

Among the reasons for the lack of high-dose chemotherapy include low-reimbursement rates and the fact that surgeons are primarily responsible for cancer treatments rather than oncologists who are knowledgeable about high-dose chemotherapeutic techniques.

Figure 21. Cancer mortality (male)

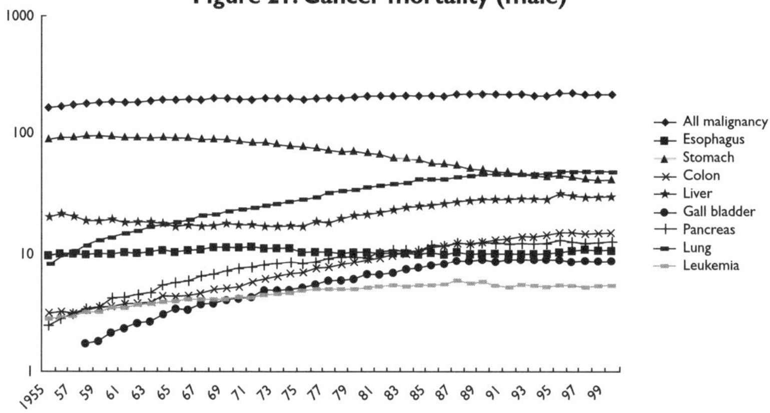

PERSPECTIVE A:

JAPAN IS USING APPROPRIATE CANCER TREATMENTS

There is a tendency in the West to use high-dose treatments to fight cancer whereas here in Japan we choose lower-dose alternatives. There are many reasons for this, but you can rest assured that cost is not a significant factor in the decision-making process. The fact is that, even for the very few patients that can endure the nearly intolerable effects of high-dose chemo, the cure rates are not very high. The other fact is that for the vast majority of patients who are not cured, their final days are lived in unnecessary pain and discomfort.

This issue may be more cultural than one of medicine or science. While many people might choose a high-dose alternative if their physician suggested that it offered an increased chance of survival, it could also be argued that there are better and more humane ways of handling such situations. Experience tells us that most patients are not in any position or condition to psychologically or emotionally understand discussions about treatment-variance statistics – especially under such trying circumstance. Clearly, critics might say that failing to appraise a patient of the statistical probabilities of one treatment over another places doctors too close to the role of God and that such a situation is intolerable. The fact is, however, that whether we like it or not, doctors do play God in every decision they make that potentially affects life or death, health or sickness. And they make a lot of such decisions. Since this is the case, why should the treatment of cancer be different than any other medical decision?

Finally, let us talk economics. As a society we need to look at the costs associated with any treatment. Ask yourself this question: would you rather pay $250,000 for 10,000 women to get PAP smears and possibly prevent cervical cancer or spend the same sum for treating with high-dose chemotherapy a single lung cancer patient that has a 20% best case chance of survival? These are the kinds of issues that all healthcare systems face. Japan has chosen well.

PERSPECTIVE B:

JAPAN USES LOWER-DOSE TREATMENTS SIMPLY TO SAVE MONEY

Cancer patients want to know what their options are and find out the relative percentages of success for each option before making a decision about treatment. You would surely want the same. If someone chooses high-dose chemotherapy and is willing to go through the pain for a better chance of survival, then that is the decision they want to be able to make and should be able to make. But, here in Japan, this option would most likely not even be presented.

There are a number of reasons why high-dose chemotherapy is not readily available in Japan. First of all, many Japanese hospitals lack the equipment and training for high-dose chemo. Furthermore, infection control standards are poor, which means there is better chance of acquiring a secondary infection. This factor is especially true since hospitalization during the treatments is required in Japan even though cancer patients in Western countries receive chemotherapy on an out-patient basis.

Japanese policy-makers and medical professionals need to change their attitude. Whether we are Japanese or not, it is an individual's decision – and it should be their right – to choose whatever gives them the best chance of beating cancer. And, in many cases, high-dose chemotherapy provides the best chance. But, to make sure that chance is made the best of, we need properly trained specialists to administer the treatment. We will also need facilities that accommodate the special demands of this patient group. But, most of all, we need to be given the right to hear the truth from our physicians.

4. HOSPICE CARE

With its aging population, Japan is experiencing more deaths among the elderly than ever before. Disturbingly, many seniors are dying at home, alone. In other cases, they face death in hospital rooms. While there is general agreement on the need for hospice care, different perspectives focus on contrasting elements of the problem.

PERSPECTIVE A:

HOSPICE CARE IS BADLY NEEDED

Death is a natural part of life and society has a responsibility to help its citizens through the dying process as much as it does with any living process. It is natural that most of us would prefer to die at home surrounded by our loved ones. The current reality of Japanese society, however, is that small family sizes and the widespread geographic distribution of families means that more and more people are dying alone. Furthermore, even when family is close at hand, the burden of caring for even dying loved ones can be emotionally and physically overwhelming.

A strong gender bias must also be considered in regard to hospice care. Japanese females live, on average, over ten years longer than their husbands. Exacerbating the situation, men tend to marry younger women and the result is that women are increasingly spending their golden years alone even if infirm and unable to care for themselves. The current lack of hospice care condemns such people to miserable conditions as they end their lives, a situation that is sad and desperately in need of improvement.

As our society ages, more and more of our citizens will need some kind of support in their final days. We need to devote some financial resources to the creation of publicly-funded hospice care centers. It is a crime to leave these once hardworking and upstanding citizens to spend their final days alone and without care.

PERSPECTIVE B:

HOSPICE CARE IS NOT AS NECESSARY AS YOU THINK

Death, to state the obvious, is unpleasant. Support as we near the end, however, is one of the few methods at our disposal to try and make these tough times better. In an ideal world, society would take charge and make certain that hospice facilities were provided to one and all for when the time comes. But resources, as we know, are becoming increasingly scarce and because this is the case, balance must be achieved and compromises made. The cost of caring for a group that no longer adds value to society must be aligned with the needs of a younger population that provides value now or in the near future. Although such ideas may sound callous to some, idealism is a luxury best practiced when resources are plentiful. Nature, unfortunately, is both callous and lacking in idealism. How we handle such realities is merely a question of how we balance our priorities – and balance is always difficult.

Another issue surrounding hospice care is, I believe, a cultural one relating to the historically Buddhist culture of Japan, a culture that values self-sacrifice and the good of the group over the individual. There is a strong case to be made that most Japanese people of the generation closest to the end of their lives have proven themselves to be self-sacrificing and focused on the betterment of society as a whole. While most may wish to be cared for, many would also reject this care if it were to appear selfish and be to the detriment of the younger generations. Who knows if this selflessness will pass on to current and future generations, but, for the time being, the culture of sacrifice is still present and a factor in the debate about care for the old and dying.

When talking about hospice care, we must not forget about the mentally challenged, a definition that could include those with severe dementia, Alzheimer's disease, and/or congenital defects affecting cognitive processes. People afflicted with such maladies need significant levels of care, particularly in the final stages of their afflictions. Society, surely, must be responsible for all its citizens so it is imperative that services be made available to everyone who is truly needy. Moreover, since these kinds of patients are relatively limited in number, the cost to the system should not overburden anyone.

While no one can argue that providing hospice services is anything but right and kind, we should not go overboard and do so at the expense of current and future generations.

5. CLINICAL LABORATORIES

Clinical laboratories are the places where blood, urine, and other pathology samples are sent to get tested. Technology has progressed to the point where many lab procedures are automated and results are available to physicians quickly and with high degrees of accuracy. Timely results can greatly help doctors make better diagnoses and prescribe appropriate treatments.

One of the biggest issues in clinical laboratory medicine in Japan is the debate surrounding the efficiencies of centralized testing in a commercial independent laboratory vs. testing done onsite at hospitals. As with many aspects of healthcare in Japan, the deciding factor seems to be economics and levels of reimbursement.

The undeniable truth is that large reference laboratories can collect clinical specimens nationwide, batch them, and run the batches on large-scale automated equipment at a fraction of the cost of processing them in small batches at local hospitals. In recent years, the shift to large-batch testing has been significant enough for the MHLW to make major reimbursement cuts related to the average cost of performing such tests. In 2001, diagnostic testing reimbursement decreased by an average of 14%. In April 2003 reimbursement was reduced by an additional 15%. This self-perpetuating cycle should drive prices down and send increasing amounts of testing to centralized testing labs. As reimbursement continues to drop, however, doing even emergency-type testing that needs to take place inside hospitals to facilitate reasonable turnaround times is becoming increasingly financially disadvantageous for hospitals. As a result, hospitals have even started sending out emergency testing at the sacrifice of turnaround time. In some places, it seems clear, deals will be made where centralized testing labs run hospitals labs on behalf of the hospital. *(Please also see Chapter 6, Section 8, Hospital Department Outsourcing.)*

A significant diagnostic manufacturing industry has emerged over the past thirty years. This industry has helped push the advances in laboratory medicine and the attendant clinical benefits. Many fear – probably quite rightly – that the decreasing financial incentives will greatly limit future investment in diagnostic medicine and even force an increasing number of companies to stop selling their products in Japan.

PERCEPTION A:
CURRENT LABORATORY TRENDS ARE POSITIVE

The only disadvantage to centralized testing vs. hospital-based testing is slower turnaround time. Even this disadvantage is being minimized with new advances in electronic-based communications, however. These days, centralized testing labs can batch tens of thousands of samples and process them at nearly one-tenth the cost of a hospital lab.

It is also arguable that there is a significant quality gap in favor of reference lab testing when compared with testing done in a hospital. While some hospitals may have very high standards, there are others with consistently poor results. Moreover, hospital labs are not accredited and neither are most of them inspected by any outside body. In contrast, most centralized labs participate in the government '*maru-teki* mark' inspection program and apply voluntarily for the College of American Pathologist (CAP) accreditation standard. The new ISO15189 standard for clinical laboratory medicine is also gaining rapid acceptance with central labs. Hardly any hospital labs participate in these kinds of programs.

For better overall quality at a tenth of the cost, slower turnaround time is a highly acceptable downside.

PERCEPTION B:
CURRENT TRENDS IN THE CLINICAL LABORATORY ARE SHORTSIGHTED AND ECONOMICALLY UNSOUND

For clinical testing results to have value for a clinician, results need to be available quickly. The doctor must also understand how to interrupt these results so as to positively affect treatment. Without these two conditions, any money spent on clinical testing is wasted.

Some tests are suitable for sending out to centralized labs, while others must be done in hospitals because of time sensitivity or other issues. Unfortunately, the current trend is to send as much testing as possible to commercial laboratories mainly because of government reimbursement policy. As a result, central testing labs tend to be used inappropriately. Tests used for monitoring drug levels in patients are one good example. Too-high drug levels mean toxicity and can cause severe harm or death. If drug levels are too low, however, they are ineffective and harm or death can result. In order for clinicians to prescribe proper subsequent dosages, they need test results within an hour or two. However, since the current trend is to send samples to the reference laboratory (with results usually received in twenty-four hours), the only information gained by doctors is if there was a dosage mistake. Of course, by this point the damage would have already been done. In these kinds of cases, it is arguably best to stop wasting money on testing and just guess the proper dosage since it is cheaper and just about as useful. There are many such examples, all leading to decreases in patient-care levels.

The next major issue relates to a physician's ability to use lab information correctly. Clinical labs can be – and used to be – important parts of the healthcare team. When labs get taken over by strangers and the majority of the testing is sent to a lab a long distance away, the opportunities for interaction, education, and the rapid handling of emergency situations decrease.

If the current trend continues, clinicians' ability to utilize this diagnostic information will shrink to the point where more and more inappropriate care gets delivered to the patient. This kind of situation will in turn result in medical errors that will lead to longer hospital stays, greater use of drugs, and more invasive procedures. This attempt to save small amounts of money in diagnostics may result in drastic overall increases in healthcare costs – not to mention increases in morbidity and mortality rates.

To conclude, independent reference lab-testing may cost less but it is an inappropriate direction for Japan's healthcare system. Because timeliness is everything with testing, information obtained too late from centralized labs is often worthless – which is the ultimate high cost. Furthermore, without the interaction that exists between the clinical laboratory and the clinical staff in hospitals, the value of centralized testing drops even more. Rationalized centralization is a good thing. The mass, wholesale centralization that is currently happening, on the other hand, will actually result in higher costs because of worsening outcomes.

6. CLINICAL TRIALS

Approval for new drugs and medical devices often requires clinical trials to occur in Japan. Historically this was a relatively straightforward process whereby companies would locate a high-status national university hospital-based physician in the relevant field. This doctor would then lead the clinical studies and publish the results. Based on the results and researchers' recommendations, the products would be approved for sale and an appropriate reimbursement price set. In the past, these researchers had significant financial and professional incentives to perform this work. They also had nearly total control over how the studies were designed and implemented.

In the late 1990s everything began to change. After several scandals in which patients died after receiving approved drugs in clinical trials performed by well-paid physician researchers, the practice of paying researchers was abolished. Additionally, the government took away the rights of researchers to design and enact clinical trials by themselves.

Documented informed consent is now required for all participating patients. Hospitals where clinical trials are performed must also have a working ethics committee and conform to Good Clinical Practice (GCP) guidelines. In another change, Clinical Research Organizations (CROs) have started actively supervising clinical trials on behalf of manufacturers. The cumulative effect has seen clinical-trial work go from being a prestigious, autonomous, and lucrative perk to what is now a thankless, cumbersome, voluntary burden. The only remaining benefit is the ability to publish the results of these trials, a necessary step for academic advancement.

The medical industry has been left with a conundrum. Getting new products approved requires local clinical trials but the unwillingness of researchers to participate remains a significant impediment to the approval process.

The government has responded in several ways. It has allowed companies to pay hospitals or universities where the clinical trials are performed. Some of these funds many now be transferred – in a transparent manner – to the department and researcher(s) leading the trials. There have also been moves to recognize foreign clinical data in certain cases where safety and efficacy are concerned, although not for reimbursement consideration. The MHLW has also approved the use of CROs, abandoning the requirement that all firms manage the clinical-trial process independently. Lastly, efforts have been made to remove the grip that national hospitals have on clinical trials and allow private hospitals to participate as well. These moves have cleared the log-jam somewhat, but clinical trials remain a formidable obstacle in the regulatory process.

One of the biggest changes in the clinical-trial world has been the new role for CROs. These companies train and employ clinical researchers to design, guide, and monitor clinical trials on a fee-for-service basis. While paid by the medical company seeking approval, some observers believe that these companies tend to provide more objective data. CROs have greatly enhanced the ability for companies to perform clinical trials and seek approvals.

PERSPECTIVE A:

CHANGES IN THE CLINICAL-TRIAL RULES HAVE GREATLY INCREASED PATIENT SAFETY AND HAVE HELPED KEEP INFERIOR PRODUCTS OUT OF THE MARKET

Clinical-trial practices in Japan needed changing. The government has done a good job by increasing the transparency of the process, and by increasing the safety for patients who participate. Better clinical trials also mean that new products are not only safe, but also effective.

At the same time, it is clear that these changes have increased the burden on both researchers and on the medical companies paying for the trials. While one can sympathize, there was no way that Japanese society could tolerate a system where doctors were paid to approve drugs. We just could not stand by and watch a system in which patients were part of clinical trials without knowing it or were – at best – poorly informed. The final insult is that products with dubious efficacy were routinely approved. Whatever new burdens have been placed on these profit-driven stakeholders, they are a small price to pay for a more rational, accountable, and transparent system.

The biggest concerns related to the regulatory changes are that the burdens placed on good clinicians are so onerous, and the cost to companies so high, that much-needed medical technologies may not be made available to Japanese patients soon enough. Such a situation is of course intolerable and we need a better system in place to ensure that the necessary incentives are made available. In fact, such changes are already happening. Universities can now have funds transferred to research departments. Further steps, however, need to be taken to motivate the best clinicians to participate in clinical trials.

PERSPECTIVE B:

CHANGES IN THE CLINICAL-TRIAL RULES WERE NECESSARY, BUT THEY HAVE GONE TOO FAR AND HAVE THE HIDDEN AGENDA OF BLOCKING THE APPROVAL OF NEW PRODUCTS JUST TO SAVE MONEY

There is no question that the old clinical-trial system needed to change. What has emerged from these changes, however, has not satisfied the overall goal of improving the safety and efficiency of healthcare. All that the new rules have done is to raise the bar for product approval so high that, as a result, some vital technologies may never reach the patients for whom they were intended. For those products eventually gaining approval, moreover, the process will take significantly longer. Not only do some of these technologies hold the promise to improve patient care, they also can add efficiencies and save on the overall cost of care delivery. Therefore, it is clear that delaying or negating these technologies through overly-burdensome clinical-trial regulations will have an overall negative impact on Japan's healthcare system.

Critics say that regulatory delays are by design. It is very possible that, in their heart of hearts, MHLW bureaucrats believe that technology drives costs up. They seem incapable of understanding the efficiencies brought about by medical technology and the positive economic as well as quality impact these technologies may have.

Whatever the motivation, the new rules have been very effective in limiting the flow of new technology into Japan. If the government is serious about achieving its goals of increased transparency and accountability without curtailing the flow of new technology, it needs to look at ways to ensure that stakeholders have the proper incentives they need in order to participate. Clinical trials should become profit-making enterprises where hospitals compete with each other based on factors such as the quality, speed, and service they provide. Physicians should be given transparent and openly administered financial incentives based on the quality of a clinical trial, irrespective of the outcome. Training should also be provided to physicians on how to handle the sensitive issue of informed consent and, as a way of alleviating this burden, trained and qualified counselors could take on a significant amount of this task. Companies should be allowed and encouraged to advertise for and pay clinical trial participants. Finally, the bureaucrats that oversee the process and the resulting data should have training and technical education adequate enough for them to be able to understand the technical and clinical implications of trial results.

Clinical trials, when done well, will always be difficult, expensive, and tedious. But, they can also be a profitable source of income for cash-strapped hospitals and physicians. Incentives must be created and maintained to ensure the proper flow of new and advanced medicines and technologies into Japan.

6 The Medical Industry

1. THE JAPANESE PHARMACEUTICAL INDUSTRY

The pharmaceutical industry is one of the largest and most profitable in the world. It is also one of the most research-intensive and costly to operate. In Japan, the pharmaceutical industry is quite unique in many ways. First of all, nearly 30% of all healthcare expenditures in Japan are on drugs in comparison with 10% to 12% in other countries. The industry here is also unique because of the large number of local pharmaceutical companies whose primary market is their home country – Japan. In fact, for the hundred or so large and medium-sized pharmaceutical companies operating in Japan, over 80% of their income is derived from Japan.

The reason for the large number of local competitors and their local emphasis is a result of government policy which lasted from the early 1960s though to the early 1990s. This policy was to promote the growth and development of pharmaceutical companies by allowing them relatively easy access to the national healthcare reimbursement system. This policy, however, unwittingly promoted the extensive prescribing of drugs. The effect snowballed when it became apparent to doctors that they, too, could make money from the large-scale sale of drugs to patients.

In many ways this policy was very successful in its day by accomplishing its stated goal of boosting the economy and promoting job growth. It also had, however, the unfortunate side effect of limiting the competitiveness of most of these firms to within their own borders. Now that government funds are drying up, the technology-hungry and battle-hardened foreign firms that succeeded in tough markets with efficacious products are cutting deeply into local competition.

What happens next? Does the government allow these technologically moribund Japanese companies to die a natural death by removing their ineffective products from the reimbursement lists and allowing foreign firms to dominate one of the world's largest industries? The impact of such a move on employment and the already sagging economy would be staggering. What should be done with the pharmaceutical industry in Japan? Let us look at some perspectives on this highly contentious issue.

PERSPECTIVE A:

THE JAPANESE PHARMACEUTICAL INDUSTRY IS A DIAMOND IN THE ROUGH. IT SHOULD BE NURTURED TO HEALTH AND THEN ALLOWED TO COMPETE GLOBALLY

The Japanese pharmaceutical industry is in some ways one of the oldest in Japan. Many of these Japanese firms have roots dating back hundreds of years ago to the time when great physician families adopted and commercialized Chinese herbal cures. In the post-war rebuilding of Japan, the government needed drugs for its national healthcare scheme and it also needed jobs for its people. Policies were therefore enacted that made it profitable to establish and grow pharmaceutical firms. These policies were successful in every way imaginable.

The government now seems too concerned about exploding healthcare costs to worry about the firms their policies created. Changes in government philosophy combined with increased pressure from foreign competitors who have massive resources from worldwide market share has meant hard times for many of these Japanese companies. If the current trend continues, many of these firms will fold. On the other hand, if they are nurtured in new and innovative ways, they can rise up and compete head-on with their foreign rivals.

Some people believe that *laissez-faire* capitalism is the only way for an economy to succeed. These people would say that Japan should throw its pharmaceutical companies to the dogs and let them live or die based solely on market dynamics. Such a policy would be tragic and misguided. Instead, the government should enact plans designed to bring the pharmaceutical industry back to health. The country, after all, still needs drugs, jobs, and exports. While many of these companies certainly need help, the industry remains relatively strong and is certainly salvageable. The benefits from salvage efforts certainly outweigh the risks.

Here's what needs to be done:

1) Stop the wholesale annual decreases in drug reimbursement levels and keep capital flowing into company coffers, at least for the time being.
2) Give tax and reimbursement incentives to drugs manufactured in Japan. Foreign governments may cry foul, but this is a national emergency and must be treated as one.
3) Give tax and reimbursement incentives so that Japanese pharmaceutical companies are motivated to merge. These mergers should be done in a way so that technical and market expertise can be augmented.
4) Stop the move towards a prospective payment reimbursement system (DPC). If DPC is adopted, it should exclude pharmaceutical products.

In a few years, after companies have had time to react to these changes, a more radical and punitive approach can be contemplated. But to sacrifice the pharmaceutical industry now, simply to save a bit of money for the national healthcare system, is throwing out the baby with the bath-water.

PERSPECTIVE B:

THE JAPANESE PHARMACEUTICAL INDUSTRY IS DYING. PUT IT OUT OF ITS MISERY

The majority of Japanese drug companies simply cannot compete with the global pharmaceutical giants of today. The inequities are overwhelming in terms of world market share and research money. With the national health scheme looking to save money, it will have no choice but to cut back on the $100 billion spent annually on drugs. When these cost-cutting policies are fully implemented, and reimbursement rates are lowered even further, the last bastion of sustainable sales and profits will be gone. When the prospective payment system inevitably goes into effect and the economic disincentives of over-prescribing are felt by hospitals, with some noteworthy exceptions the era of powerful Japanese pharmaceutical companies will be over.

There is no question that the decline of Japan's drug industry will hurt the already faltering economy and cost jobs. Of course this is not a good thing but it is also a reality that needs facing. To try and prop up these firms with artificial market incentives will simply increase the overall financial woes of the healthcare system and do nothing more than stave off the inevitable collapse of these companies.

What needs to be done is clear. Focus on patient-centered healthcare reforms, not industry-focused ones. Enact a prospective payment system as soon as practicable. Then, let companies compete by the only meaningful standard reasonable – the value to patients.

The result will be strong companies rising up to create real value for the healthcare system even though, inevitably, weaker firms, will collapse and die. Others will diversify into areas where they can effectively compete. What is irrefutable is that the overall condition of the healthcare system outweighs the importance of a few companies in one industry sector. There simply is not enough room for government-protected markets to exist any longer in today's global economy.

2. THE MEDICAL EQUIPMENT AND SUPPLY INDUSTRY

Medical equipment and devices include a wide range of products. At one end of the spectrum, these products include artificial heart valves, stents, catheters, and medical imaging equipment. At the other end are wound dressings and examination gloves. In the past, most of these products were reimbursed each time hospitals used them. This range was a driving force behind the huge medical distribution business that once consisted of over 6,000 independent distributors. Because of this huge network, these kinds of products were never stocked. Instead, they were ordered every time they were needed, a just-in-time system that was popular with many hospitals and clinics.

Things have changed a great deal in recent years. Many older drug products are no longer eligible for individual reimbursements and have been relegated to the general supply category. This situation is especially true for the common-use, lower-tech, commodity-type of products. Prior to this reclassification, everyone with a direct stake in care delivery had an incentive to keep these products priced as high as possible because hospitals profited from every product purchased. But, now that these same products have been placed in a general supply category, they have become a cost instead of a revenue producer.

There has also been downward pricing pressure for reimbursed products. These price decreases happen during periodic governmental price reviews. Prior to these reviews, the government compels all medical distributors to disclose pricing data and new prices are set in accordance with the analysis of these surveys. In the past, it was to everyone's advantage to ensure that these surveys showed 'market forces' driving prices up; therefore product reimbursements would increase. In actuality, however, the true marketplace was full of discounts in the form of free goods and other questionable practices. While this cozy system worked well for all concerned (except, of course, the government treasury), it also helped create some of the highest prices in the world for many classes of medical products.

This method for setting reimbursement rates was not the only reason that prices for medical products were considerably higher in Japan than in other markets. Intrinsic demands from hospitals and Japan's medical profession in general also contributed to a high cost of doing business. Multiple distribution channels, lavish entertainment of doctors, excessive service requirements, overly burdensome regulatory requirements – all of these factors were unique to Japan and created costs unseen in other markets around the world.

With an eye to cutting costs, the government is now looking towards something called foreign-reference pricing. This practice would extend pricing surveys outside Japan to include other markets – especially a manufacturer's home market. While manufacturers are keen to point to the high cost of doing business in Japan, the government is much more concerned about their looming budget shortfalls.

PERSPECTIVE A:

THE MEDICAL INDUSTRY IS BEING UNFAIRLY SINGLED OUT. THE GOVERNMENT DOES NOT RECOGNIZE THE VALUE AND COST SAVINGS THESE TECHNOLOGIES YIELD TO THE SYSTEM

Medical equipment and supplies account for only 7% of all medical expenditures in Japan. Yet, it seems that the MHLW spends 90% of its time trying to bring down the cost of these products, mainly by adapting the irrational process of foreign-reference pricing that does not take into account the extremely high cost of doing business in Japan. While the government pushes through these reimbursement decreases, it is also doing nothing to streamline the business environment. On the contrary, it is increasing an already-excessive regulatory burden. For example, the government has made it much more difficult to get new products registered, let alone reimbursed. And, when products do get registered, the higher value (and typically higher cost) products are cast off into the non-reimbursed, highly advanced category.

The technologies that have been brought to market over the past thirty years have been very advantageous to both the system and to patients. These technologies have also contributed greatly to improved mortality rates. Examples of technologies that have improved patient care include long-lasting pacemakers as small as a watch, balloon catheters which reduce the need for surgical procedures, stents to unblock arteries, medical imaging devices which virtually eliminate the need for exploratory surgeries, and laparoscopic procedures – to name but a few. Without these types of products the medical profession would lack essential and important tools and would be required to do more invasive procedures, increasing the financial cost as well as the cost in human lives.

The policies of the Japanese government have failed to recognize the value of medical technology. Cost-cutting has become the holy grail and the result has meant negative effects on both the quality and the price of healthcare delivery. Many of the most advanced medical products are in regulatory limbo so that patients cannot enjoy their benefits. Regulatory problems aside, the reimbursement of these newer products has been classified with older versions, which means that there is no economic incentive to create new or innovative products. Foreign medical companies are increasingly choosing to bypass Japan or simply give distribution rights for new products to importers and let them deal with the problems.

Medical technologies need to be reimbursed by the value they bring to patients. Local economic conditions must also be taken into account. If Japan wants to enjoy the benefits of medical technology both now and in the future, the practice of foreign-reference pricing must also be abandoned. Instead, the government must look at the root cause of Japan's higher prices, which are regulatory burdens and the high cost of customer service and distribution.

New advances in technologies that bring efficiencies, cost savings, or advances in the quality of medical care must be rewarded with reimbursements higher than those of old-generation products. If a prospective payment system (DPC) is adopted, advanced medical technologies must be exempt from it. They should also be reimbursed separately, at least in the early stages, to mitigate high research costs and the price of bringing a new product to market. Lastly, when evaluating reimbursement rates, the government needs to start recognizing the potential labor savings that many of these technologies foster.

The government is looking towards foreign-reference pricing as a rational way of calculating new reimbursement prices. Not only does this fail to take into account the high cost of doing business in Japan, it also ignores the efficiencies of other medical systems. For example, in the United States, hospital groups order hundreds of devices at a time, allowing manufacturers to base their prices on an economy of scale. In Japan, medical manufacturers are often forced to sell similar products one at a time. Should not government bureaucrat understand the economics and the associated pricing of selling products in bulk vs. single sales?

Failure to recognize the value of new technologies through the medium of higher reimbursement means that it will be increasingly difficult for Japanese patients to receive the benefits of these technologies. Such a failure also means that the healthcare system will not receive the cost and productivity benefits that such new technologies offer. If the government remains myopically focused on chipping away at the 7% of healthcare funds spent on medical equipment, the savings will be extremely small and very temporary – not to mention the negative effects on patient care.

The government has to refocus away from the trivial and concentrate on the real problems: excess hospital beds, overly long hospital stays, and the overuse of pharmaceutical products. Perhaps the biggest problem of all, however, is a political one; it may well be that medical device companies are being sacrificed because they lack the political strength of the JMA and other groups that are responsible for most healthcare spending.

PERSPECTIVE B:

PRICES HAVE BEEN TOO HIGH FOR TOO LONG AND IT IS ABOUT TIME THEY CAME DOWN TO WORLD NORMS

There has been an ongoing conspiracy between medical manufacturers, distributors, hospitals, and doctors to set and maintain high prices for medical equipment in Japan. Such a situation was tolerable when Japan had a younger, less medically burdensome population. However, given the current demographic trends and general economic doldrums, all areas of medicine need to be reviewed critically and sacrifices must be made. No one denies the value these new technologies bring to patients. But, there is also no denying that many of these technologies cost three to five times more in Japan than they do in other countries. Industry says the reason for these cost levels is the high cost of doing business in Japan. Although there is no doubt that this is part of the problem, it is a really just a simple chicken-or-egg situation. Are the costs of doing business so high because Japan is expensive, or did these costs grow out of the excess profits resulting from high prices?

Regardless of why prices are so high, they must come down. If, in fact, the general business environment is costly, it will need to evolve and adapt to these new realities. Industry always looks to government to change the business environment prior to price rationalization. The question then is, what practical steps can the government take to change this environment – besides, that is, cutting down on excess profit-taking and letting the changes flow from there?

The implementation of a prospective payment system (DPC) will give new technologies the value they deserve through improved productivity and advances in patient care. DPC will take time, however, to permeate the entire marketplace. In the meantime the government needs to find a rational way to lower costs. Because of the cozy relationships between hospitals, dealers, and manufacturers, the farce of artificially high pricing surveys is not going to go away soon. Instead, the only rational method for equitably cutting reimbursement prices is to do research in other markets and set prices accordingly. Of course, small premiums may be added for export products and the added costs of doing business in Japan – but nothing more.

This next issue is one that is often thought of, but seldom mentioned. Difficult as it is to say, healthcare, by necessity, must be rationed. Of course we all want the best healthcare technology can provide. But, there are also economic realities that need to be considered. In the Japanese system, which is focused on the fair and equitable application of its healthcare resourses, tough decisions are a reality. One of these tough realities is that some technologies are simply unaffordable right now. Hopefully, over time, as technologies get older and become more accepted and cheaper, they can be added when they become economically viable.

3. THE DIAGNOSTIC INDUSTRY

The diagnostic industry refers to the business of testing blood, urine, and body tissues for hundreds of different disease indicators. In the industry – and for our purposes – diagnostics are referred to as In-vitro-diagnostics (IVD). IVD tests can be performed in the clinical lab of a hospital or sent out to central reference laboratories. Recent technologies even allow some tests to be performed at a patient's bedside.

Physician use the results of diagnostic tests to diagnose patients for diseases and to screen seemingly healthy patients for early-stage diseases. The goal is to treat patients pre-symptomatically. When caught early, many diseases such as cancer are treated more successfully than if found later. Early-stage treatment is also arguably more cost effective.

When compared with other healthcare industry sectors, the diagnostic industry is unique in several ways. First, substantial diagnostic testing (mainly in the form of health checks known as *ningen dokku*) already takes place outside the reimbursed national healthcare scheme. These health checks are done at periodical intervals, and are often paid for by employers or, increasingly, by individuals themselves. There are over ten million health checks done annually in Japan and most health check centers are run fully for-profit. What is more, a large number of not-for-profit hospitals have opened for-profit facilities to capitalize on this lucrative opportunity.

The second thing that makes the IVD industry unique is that it is the only area of hospital services involving patient care that can be outsourced to for-profit subcontractors. The reason this kind of service is possible is because subcontractors have no direct contact with patients other than their tissues, blood, or other bodily fluids; as a result the JMA – which strongly opposes the outsourcing of medical services to for-profit entities – has let this situation escape their radar screen.

As with the pharmaceutical industry, the domestic IVD industry has flourished under the public policies of the past thirty years. There are well over one hundred domestic companies who manufacture and sell the chemical reagents and/or instrumentation systems necessary for diagnostic testing. Paralleling the pharmaceutical industry again, the lion's share of new advances in IVD testing come from multinational companies with worldwide markets and large R&D budgets and not from their Japanese counterparts who depend mostly on domestic sales.

The diagnostic industry is facing tremendous challenges of late. The most noteworthy of these is rapidly-falling prices. Unlike some other areas, IVD testing tends not to be reimbursed at rates significantly higher than those of other industrialized countries. So, from a lower starting point, the industry has suffered deep reimbursement cuts exceeding 10% to 12% at the bi-annual pricing revisions.

The reason that the government can rationalize such high cuts in reimbursement is because, as reimbursement decreases, there is less incentive for hospitals to perform the tests themselves. Thus, hospitals send more tests to central testing labs. These central testing laboratories use comparatively large economies of scale to achieve testing results for less money. Competition among commercial labs ensures that these efficiencies are passed on to the end-user in the form of lower prices. Of course, when the government does its pricing surveys, a clear decrease in price can be seen and which the government feels compelled to reflect in the revised reimbursement rates. This self-defeating cycle, some claim, threatens the entire IVD industry in Japan.

PERSPECTIVE A:

IVD TESTING HAS BEEN OVERUSED IN THE PAST. CURRENT TRENDS ARE POSITIVE FOR THE HEALTHCARE SYSTEM AS A WHOLE

In-vitro diagnostic testing (IVD) is a key tool in the practice of medicine regardless of country. The problem with IVD, however, is that a relatively high percentage of testing is done more for monetary gain than for the value of the information it provides. Like so much of the economics of healthcare in Japan, this situation has been brought about historically by policy-makers who focused on the administration of healthcare no less than they focused on creating jobs and an industry with its resultant economic benefits. Although these past policies were very successful at creating a domestic diagnostic industry, unfortunately it was at the expense of healthcare economics.

The government policies mentioned above resulted in the creation of hundreds of manufacturers and distributors of diagnostic products. This success was brought about mainly due to the former, rather loose, regulatory environment that focused more on safety than on efficacy. Because IVD testing occurs outside the human body, safety is a relatively simple issue and Japan now boasts the largest number of approved tests in the world. For example, Japan has approved nearly one hundred cancer markers alone compared to the mere half-dozen that have met American FDA requirements.

It has been clearly demonstrated that as long as these tests are reimbursed – regardless of efficacy – physicians will order them. And why not? They certainly do no harm and should result in increased revenues for doctors and hospitals.

In this increasingly tight fiscal environment how can one separate the wheat from the chaff? Who is going to determine which assays have value, and which have been approved simply to build a domestic diagnostic industry on the back of the national healthcare scheme? These questions are not easy ones, but the answers likely lie in the new prospective payment scheme known in Japan as DPC.

Theoretically, diagnostics can speed up the diagnosis process and ensure that the diagnosis is correct. Both of these factors lead to more effective treatment and quicker recovery. A prospective payment system like DPC rewards those hospitals that diagnose most effectively and gain the best outcomes. Obviously, for hospitals to succeed under this program, it will be important for them to use the right IVD tests effectively. If DPC is properly administered the effective IVDs should flourish and the ineffective one disappear.

The same argument about effective vs. ineffective applies to the debate about using centralized reference labs in place of hospital laboratories. The main reason for hospital testing, clearly, is speed. Tests that need turnaround of less then twenty-four hours should be done in hospitals. When test results are not needed quickly, the testing can be done more efficiently in large reference labs thanks to their economies of scale. An effectively administered DPC system should provide hospitals with ready incentives to make this determination based on the best patient outcomes. Surely such a selection process is preferable to the current system where these kind of allocation decisions are sometimes made simply by calculating profit margins.

The key to the success of the diagnostic industry is doctors' understanding how to use and interpret test results. Because technology progresses so quickly, it is very difficult for clinicians to understand and use every type of result to assign the optimal therapy. In the best interests of the payers, the patients, and IVD industry, effective information and education programs must find their way to the types of physicians who have historically focused on therapeutics.

PERSPECTIVE B:

CURRENT TRENDS IN DIAGNOSTICS ARE HAVING A DEVASTATING EFFECT ON PATIENT CARE AND WILL ULTIMATELY COST THE SYSTEM ECONOMICALLY

Most physicians say that diagnosing a patient is the most difficult part of practicing medicine. Once a definitive diagnosis has been made, treatment options are typically well established. The IVD industry has given physicians unprecedented tools to help with diagnoses as well as for monitoring treatment effectiveness. To date, the fee-for-service system has effectively been the driving force behind doctors learning new testing procedures. For all intents and purposes this system has worked as an education program, financially motivating doctors who understand which tests to order under which circumstances.

The IVD industry's greatest fear is that, in the blind march to a prospective payment system (DPC), the motivation to stay informed will be removed and will not be replaced. The result could be an irrational decrease in IVD testing – to the determent of patients. The theory behind DPC is well understood: that the system will promote the most effective use of medical tools, including IVDs. The reality is, however, that while this incentive may well exist, physicians will increasingly rely on empirical clinical data rather than spending money on tests. This fear is supported by the lack of negative motivators. In other countries, for example, doctors can be sued for malpractice if they fail to order proper tests when circumstances indicate they are necessary.

The issue of central reference lab testing vs. hospital testing is not merely about say, the cost of a certain reagent when purchased in bulk. It goes much deeper. The central issue is that effective healthcare is a team effort and the captain of this team is certainly the doctor. But for the captain to run the team he or she needs to have access to a pharmacist so that drug interactions are covered. He or she also needs to talk to the nurses who spend so much time with the patient. And, yes, he or she must also interface with the lab, which is especially true with new and complex diagnostic tests that can be confusing and difficult to interpret. If this testing is being sent off-site and the tests performed by unknown people, the entire team dynamic is lost. The losers will be the hospital, for one – which will increasingly be tasked with providing quality outcomes – and, of course, the patient, whose care will be negatively affected.

If certain vested interests are successful and the majority of IVD testing gets sent to reference labs, the result will be a wholesale destruction of the diagnostic industry. Funds for further R&D will dry up and the system will lose the benefits that new technologies bring. As we stand at the brink of new discoveries in molecular biology where the root genetic causes of disease can be deciphered, the implications for IVD testing are profound.

The current direction being followed by Japanese policy-makers is potentially very destructive. Policies to bring reimbursement levels below global norms will result in the decreased use of important products. Slower and/or missed diagnoses will occur followed, possibly, by improper or ineffective treatments leading to poorer patient care at an increased cost. Implementing prospective payments without replacing the current testing incentives will also lead to the underutilization of IVD procedures with the same outcome as mentioned above.

Prior to implementing a prospective payment system, the government needs to reimburse IVDs adequately. A dual pricing system (one for hospital testing and one for reference lab testing) must be put in place that recognizes that it is more expensive to run tests in hospitals and that it can be advantageous to do so. When prospective payments become the norm in Japan, the system should insist that IVD testing results be made available on demand to ensure that proper diagnoses – and proper billing codes – have been made.

4. THE MEDICAL SERVICES INDUSTRY

The medical services industry is a difficult industry to define since, in fact, all of healthcare is a service provided to patients. Medical services in Japan could be defined as a for-profit business that supplies hospitals, doctors, or patients with auxiliary services directly relating to patient care. This definition is particularly important because, to a large extent, the companies just described cannot render these types of services under existing laws. Current laws stipulate that virtually all work done directly to and for patients must be done exclusively by physicians.

Some rules, however, have been loosened in recent years. In 2002, regulations were finally relaxed, giving nurses the legal right to give injections or connect IVs. The biggest changes in the law, however, have been brought about by the home healthcare system, established in 2001. This law gave private, for-profit companies the ability to provide healthcare support to the elderly at home, away from the physician's watchful eye.

While there has been positive movement in allowing for-profit companies into this potentially lucrative services sector, there are also significant barriers. Most of these barriers concern physician autonomy over everything connected to patient care.

Industry backers argue that the private sector can bring increased efficiencies and deliver higher quality healthcare for less money. Areas which might become available to the private sector and are currently being debated include:

a) Hospital ownership by for-profit companies
b) Outsourcing of essential hospital services
c) Home drug-infusion therapies
d) Telemedicine Services Opponents, however, are quick to point to the negatives of treating the patient as an 'object' passed around to different organizations that have little or no physician oversight.

Based on experiences in Western countries, there seems little question that medical services as defined above can offer significant advantages. But, the real question is: can it work in Japan? Below are some perspectives on the subject.

PERSPECTIVE A:

LAWS LIMITING MEDICAL SERVICES SHOULD BE RELAXED SO THAT THE EFFICIENCIES OF PRIVATE BUSINESS CAN HELP PROVIDE BETTER AND LESS-EXPENSIVE HEALTHCARE

There are certain healthcare service sectors that lend themselves wonderfully to private, for-profit business models. Current laws, regulations, and Japanese business practices, however, do not give private companies the chance to capitalize on what are very real business opportunities. These protectionist policies work to the detriment of a great many stakeholders – including the payers, the patients, and even the doctors and hospitals that these laws are supposed to help.

The medical services sector in Japan is poised to explode. All of the ingredients exist for a great many profitable enterprises, including:

a) A skilled, well-educated, and under-utilized workforce consisting of all kinds of medical professionals – including doctors.
b) An aging population with increasing health needs who have the ability and willingness to pay for care.
c) Increasing availability of groups and individuals with the key skill sets needed to help emerging businesses (i.e. technology skills).

Examples abound. Let us take the area of telemedicine, for instance. If regulations permitted, elderly people could subscribe to services which send healthcare providers to their homes. Pharmacy delivery services could deliver drugs and other health-support materials. Hospitals could outsource many departmental functions, including medical imaging, clinical laboratory services, rehabilitation medicine, and pharmacy services. Chronic care facilities could become assisted-living facilities which would enhance the lifestyles as well as the health of the elderly.

Capitalism is a powerful force. If private enterprises are given the chance at what they believe is a viable business opportunity, they are ready, willing, and able to set up organizations that are far more capable than what is in place now. Companies would create standardized operating systems complete with education and testing for their employees. Quality-control procedures would be put into place and business managers would constantly be seeking new ways to improve service to patients and increase productivity. Compare this to the current system where doctors – trained in science, but typically with no business or administrative training – run everything. Compare this to the current system where healthcare workers work in the cocoon of their own hospital and are seldom exposed to or allowed to try new ideas. Compare this to the typical politically-charged environment of today's Japanese healthcare facility where egos typically outweigh the need for change.

From an economic standpoint, greater efficiency translates into lower costs for the people paying the bills and – of course – profits for the companies. Greater efficiency means more jobs for workers and an environment where workers are encouraged and challenged to grow, change, and improve.

The government needs to look closely at its current policies restricting medical services companies from entering the Japanese market. Instead, they should allow private industry to compete and add value.

PERSPECTIVE B:

RELAXING MEDICAL SERVICES RULES IS A STEP THAT NEEDS TO BE SCRUTINIZED CAREFULLY. CLEAR LINES OF ACCOUNTABILITY MUST BE ESTABLISHED BEFORE ANY LIBERALIZATION OCCURS

In administering any system as complex as a hospital or other healthcare facilities, it is of paramount importance that accountability for patient well-being be clearly defined. There is no question that the person best trained to oversee quality healthcare delivery for the betterment of the patient is the physician. Current rules in Japan reflect this hierarchy by giving significant latitude to the physician in charge. It is also a tremendous responsibility.

Naysayers argue that it is better to give the responsibility for managing healthcare to people with business training rather than those with science or medical backgrounds. This kind of thinking can be dangerous and destructive. The focus of healthcare needs to be the patient and medical excellence cannot be found in a computer program or a management system. Medical care is based on the relationships between doctors and patients and between physicians and other healthcare professionals.

Modern Japanese healthcare already has enough systematization and mechanization. There have also been ample attempts to increase efficiency. Take a tour of any modern Japanese healthcare facility and you might even come away feeling that there is already too much efficiency at the expense of dehumanized patients. To let corporations buy hospitals or allow hospitals to farm out entire departments to the lowest bidder may sound good on paper. What really matters, however, are the day-to-day interactions between patients and healthcare professionals. If we are not careful we will soon be treated by robots instead of people, all for the sake of efficiency, no matter what the cost.

All things change. But change typically happens slowly and naturally and for good reason. The problem now is that the government looks at its financial woes and seems determined to ignore the natural approach to change as it rushes blindly ahead, grasping for straws in the dark. In the end, we may well arrive at the same place; but whenever change is radical and hurried, a great number of people get hurt.

We need to accommodate change. In the healthcare field, change may well extend to private companies operating healthcare facilities, hospital departments, or even businesses based on some of the new technologies that are helping redefine the field. Perhaps private companies will even be more efficient than organizations run by doctors. Regardless, change must be managed in a way that puts the best interests of the patient first. Here are some suggestions about how to do so:

1) Allow corporate hospital ownership in one area of the country on an experimental basis. Watch it closely to see if it works, how it works, and what problems occur.
2) Study the use of the Internet in so-called telemedicine. Perhaps start by letting patients request information on drug interactions over the Net.
3) Clinical lab tests are already being outsourced from hospitals to private labs. As more information about this 'experiment' becomes available, study this area and see if promised efficiencies occur and at what cost.
4) Seriously examine proposals from private industry but do not act on them until we fully understand the total impact any proposal would have on patients.

From a purely financial viewpoint, the efficiencies of private medical services may sound attractive. But we will all one day be patients. And when you are the one lying in a hospital bed or on an operating table, your perspective may well be very different.

5. MEDICAL PRODUCT DISTRIBUTION

The distribution of medical products in Japan is a complicated latticework of interlocking relationships between people, companies, and medical facilities. At one point in the 1980s, nearly 7,000 distributors of medical products and nearly 2,000 distributors of pharmaceuticals crowded the field. The number of distributors decreased rapidly during the 1990s, however, leaving only about 2,500 medical device and disposable product distributors and only 10–12 pharmaceutical wholesalers. This process of attrition took place through acquisition, no-charge transfer of businesses, or – in some cases – either bankruptcy or the voluntary closure of operations.

Figure 22. Pharma sales in Japan by distribution (US$m)

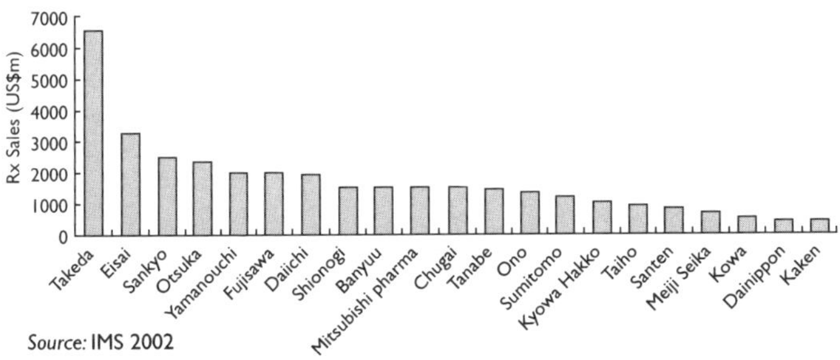

Source: IMS 2002

The driving force behind this rationalization in distributor numbers was a decrease in reimbursements. These cuts eliminated much of the 'fluff' from the system and forced businesses to look at ways to reduce costs. As such, many distributors found themselves at the bottom of the food chain, with predictable results.

Medical device and supply distributors perform a number of functions above and beyond the physical distribution of products. One of the most meaningful roles played by distributors is that of collection agency or bank. Many of these distributors have credit terms of up to six months or more with hospitals while they pay manufacturers on a net-thirty or sixty-day basis. They also play another important role as inventory controllers for hospitals. Because of the close relationship between some distributors and hospitals, many hospitals feel it unnecessary to organize and manage their own inventories. Hospitals often request the supply of a single item – and it will usually get there within twenty-four hours. These distributors even play useful roles for the government, which counts on them for regular pricing survey data.

The government has recently taken steps to stem the tide of distributors closing shop. In the past, the domestic manufacturer and/or importer of medical products could sell directly to end-users if they so desired. New regulations will demand that all sales go through a licensed local distributor. The stated reason for the new law is to ensure that all transactions can be traced more easily. Also, to promote more open competition, the government has recently made rules making it illegal for manufacturers to dictate prices to distributors. Theoretically this would allow for more pricing competition in hospital purchasing offices. It is unclear how well these rules are working, however. Regardless, the net effect of the new regulations is clear. They will result in medical dealers remaining an integral part of doing business in Japan.

There is, however, a darker side to distributors. First, there have been cases where unscrupulous firms have served as useful tools for hospitals (particularly privately-owned ones) who wanted to skim funds. One way in which these so-called 'tunnel companies' operate is by having a doctor set someone up as their main distributor. The doctor in question would then ensure that all hospital purchases get funneled through this distributor. The distributor would make a reasonable profit from these transactions and a certain amount of the 'proceeds' would be returned to said physician. Although there is nothing strictly illegal about this process, it is a much-exploited loophole whereby so-called non-profit companies make money.

Some industry observers believe that the medical distribution industry is a useless remnant of the past. Others, however, take a different tack and contend that these distributors have a valuable and significant role to play for both the practice of medicine and Japanese society.

PERSPECTIVE A:

THE MEDICAL SUPPLY DISTRIBUTION SYSTEM IS WASTEFUL AND NEEDS IMMEDIATE REFORM

Like so many of the current woes in healthcare, the distribution system for medical products in Japan resulted from government policies designed to create employment through indirect funding in the form of the national healthcare scheme. Although this situation parallels what policy-makers did when they helped create the domestic pharmaceutical, medical device, and diagnostic industries, there is a difference. Unlike those other industries, the distribution system has not resulted in any intrinsic or long-lasting value. No intellectual properties were created nor have there been any technological advances. No exportable commodities were produced either. The only thing that this system created – other than jobs – was a massive drain on a system that can no longer afford it.

Figure 23. Internationally-held companies

	Mar. 00	Mar. 01	Mar. 02
Chugai	34	43	46
Shionogi	32	39	40
Yamanouchi	39	43	40
Daiichi	26	27	32
Sankyo	31	36	30
Takeda	28	30	30
Ono	19	25	28
Santen	19	17	26
Eisai	27	28	25
Fujisawa	24	20	23
Tanabe	12	10	20
Average	**26**	**29**	**31**

Source: 'Pharma Update, Japan Sector Overview,' UBS Investment Bank, 28 July 2003

Figure 24. Japanese-controlled companies

	Mar. 00	Mar. 01	Mar. 02
Kyorin	11	13	13
Taisho	11	10	11
Dainippon	10	16	9
Meji Seka	9	6	8
Kyowa Hakko	7	7	6
Tsumura	3	2	6
Kaken	9	4	5
Hisamitsu	5	6	4
Mochida	2	2	2
Average	**7**	**7**	**7**

Source: 'Pharma Update, Japan Sector Overview,' UBS Investment Bank, 28 July 2003

At the risk of sounding obvious, a distributor's job is to physically deliver a product from point A to point B. With the excellent delivery systems available these days in Japan, anything can be delivered anywhere within twenty-four hours – if not faster. With such a superlative system already in place, there is no rational explanation as to how an army of tens of thousands with hundreds of warehouses – spread all over the country – can add any functionality whatsoever to the system. In fact, it is even possible that the sheer size of this system actually decreases its efficiency and, in some cases, actually slows delivery.

Let us be honest. The only value that medical distributors really bring is to hospital owners. Although they also take on collection risk for manufacturers and act as spies for government bureaucrats and employ thousands in make-work jobs, these activities could hardly be considered the true functions of a 'distributor.' Surely the real job of distributors is to deliver products – a function that can be accomplished with greater ease at lower cost by using one of Japan's many excellent express delivery services.

Let us be clear. Hospital owners should make money by practicing medicine, not through questionable business relationships with 'tunnel companies.' Companies should collect money from hospitals directly or, if not, they should hire a collection agency not a medical products distributor. The government is equally culpable by failing to find better ways of collecting the data they need for price surveys. Besides, with the advent of prospective payments (DPC), the government will be getting out of the price-fixing business anyway.

The toughest issue is that of employment, particularly in rural areas where being a medical representative is considered a good job. What is more, although small, rural medical distribution companies add significantly to local tax revenues. There is no easy answer. But, if the government is serious about evolving towards a more fiscally responsible and patient-centered system, jettisoning small distribution companies may well be one of the many sacrifices that must be made.

PERSPECTIVE B:
DISTRIBUTORS OF MEDICAL PRODUCTS PROVIDE A VALUABLE SERVICE TO MANUFACTURERS AND HOSPITAL AS WELL AS EMPLOYING THOUSANDS IN GOOD JOBS

It is easy to look back at past decisions and criticize them. The fact is, events and situations were different decades ago. The medical distribution environment that we are now discussing has its roots in a time when logistical systems were primitive compared to those of today. Government then was committed to creating a national healthcare system at a time when the country was coming out of post-war depression. Then, the development of the medical products distribution system was nothing short of wonderful.

Of course times change and things need to evolve. This truism applies to business as much as to life. Well, medical distribution has evolved too and the number of distributors has dropped by more than half from its peak. Employment in the system has also decreased sharply. The biggest change, however, is that the traditional job of the distributor – shifting products from point A to point B – is no longer their main role. Here are some of valuable services that medical distribution companies in Japan provide:

1) Medical distributors can act as just-in-time inventory control managers for hospitals. This valuable service ensures that products needed for patient care are available on demand, without the hospital maintaining or organizing a costly inventory system.
2) It is well known that many hospitals are in financial trouble. Many medical distributors have helped hospitals by acting as financial buffers between manufacturers – who demand immediate payment – and hospitals which need longer credit terms.
3) Medical distributors are also in a unique position *vis-à-vis* their ability to gather information in a non-partisan way. Although this potential has not been fully exploited, it is being used successfully by the government to monitor and set pricing revisions.

As you can see, distributors are useful. In addition, this industry provides tens of thousands of jobs. We need to build on something that was painstakingly constructed over time instead of throwing out the baby with the bath-water. We should support the ongoing involvement of medical distributors in Japan and help them grow and add value in new and different ways.

7 Do Solutions Exist?

1. THE MINISTRY OF HEALTH, LABOUR AND WELFARE'S GRAND SCHEME

While no one knows what lurks in the minds of MHLW bureaucrats, based on their current behavior it is pretty clear that they are up to something. From all appearances, these entrenched officials seem to be fighting what can only be called guerilla warfare. Their enemies are the economic stakeholders of vested interests in the healthcare field who are fighting tooth and nail to preserve their status quo. These enemies include not only the obvious foes such the Japan Medical Association (JMA) and the 9,000 hospitals and 90,000 clinics the JMA supports; they also extend to the domestic and multinational pharmaceutical and medical device companies that profit handsomely from the current system. The final group of enemies consists of the politicians who receive substantial contributions from the above-mentioned special-interest groups.

Looking at their powerful opposition, it is clear that the MHLW bureaucrats have their work cut out for them. Although their tactics are not fully understood, it seems that the MHLW grand scheme includes decreasing costs, improving quality, and fundamentally changing how healthcare works in Japan. Here is the plan in more detail:

1) To mandate a prospective payment system in the university hospitals – places where the JMA has no control and no economic interests.
2) To privatize university hospitals so that they care about the economic effects of the prospective payment system and do not simply remain dependent on public funds.

3) To sneak a reimbursement adjustment factor into the prospective payment system so that reimbursements will vary from hospital to hospital. Initially, this innovation will only concern length of stay and be based on reimbursements calculated on a daily basis. Hospitals with shorter patient stays will receive a higher daily rate and those with longer stays will get a lower daily rate. The key point here is that both kinds of hospitals will get the same amount of money.
4) To expand this hospital-to-hospital variance factor so it includes quality indicators. For example, a hospital that is ISO- or JCQHC-accredited will receive higher reimbursements than those that are not. Suddenly, there is a new economic incentive to install quality systems.
5) To expand the system into a larger pool of non-university hospitals in order to gradually increase quality and the effect of the new reimbursement scheme. The hospitals with the shortest stays and highest quality standards will survive. Those with the longest stays and poorest quality indicators will be gradually eliminated. Darwin would be proud.

PERSPECTIVE A:

THE MHLW PLAN IS BRILLIANT

Long time participants and observers of the Japan healthcare scene have been surprised by the MHLW plan. Frankly, when considering the entrenched political interests and the huge amounts of money at stake, most old hands thought there was no way out of this messy situation other than a complete meltdown. We are happy to say, however, that there now seems to be light at the end of the tunnel thanks to the MHLW`s recently enacted DPC system for university hospitals. Assuming that the bureaucrats can stick to their guns and keep the plan moving forward without a violent backlash from the JMA and their pet politicians, the plan has a real chance of bringing meaningful change.

DPC should not only rein in the costs associated with the fee-for-service system, it should also mean improved quality standards because of the varying reimbursement rates. While these rates now only consider length of stay, they can easily be manipulated to force hospitals to adopt quality systems. Here is what else needs to be included into the calculations: a) hospital accreditation status; b) physician residency requirements; c) Continuing Medical Education

(CME) for all medical staff; and d) giving patients access to their medical charts.

By steadily cranking up quality requirements – through either an increase in the number of complying hospitals or by decreasing reimbursement to non-complying ones – the MHLW should ultimately be able to break the backs of the most poorly performing hospitals. When that happens, the system will channel its funds to the hospitals most committed to delivering the highest quality services. This change alone will not solve the healthcare system's economic woes, to be sure, but it will certainly take the entire system in the right direction.

PERSPECTIVE B:

THIS IS NOT THE MHLW'S PLAN. DPC WILL FAIL

Everyone understands that the current healthcare system is under increasing economic strain. It is equally clear that the MHLW's job is to try and come up with solutions to these kinds of problems and provide the best care they can for the patients they are sworn to serve. This trend towards a Japanese-style prospective payment system is simply an experiment being done for political reasons and the results are easy to predict: the participating hospitals will fail to lower their care delivery costs, proving once and for all that prospective payment will not work in Japan. The reasons why it will not are multifaceted and are ingrained in Japan's history and culture. These issues are:

1) DPC has been imposed on the system without adequate consensus building. No broadly-based initiative like this succeeds without the consensus of its stakeholders.
2) In the university hospital setting, physicians are poorly paid and are already very cost-conscious as a result of their training and hospital policy. Introduction of a DPC system will simply increase their paperwork and will not change the way they treat patients.
3) Care providers in university hospitals do not usually consider cost when treating patients because they are already far removed from the financial management of the hospitals in which they work. It is unlikely that any physician will change their practice patterns as a result of the introduction of a DPC system.
4) University hospitals are either managed with public funds or are financed by large private endowments. The entire system depends on outside funding.

5) Since university hospitals get the most difficult cases they are not representative of normal hospitals. Therefore, using their data for things like treatment patterns and length of stay and then trying to extrapolate it to the larger hospital population will simply produce meaningless results. The data generated will almost certainly lead to the discarding of the entire DPC idea – which could be a mistake.
6) Most importantly, there are a large number of powerful lobbies that want this DPC experiment to fail and be kept away from private hospitals.

I applaud the MHLW`s attempts to improve the system both economically and structurally. However, this DPC experiment is doomed to fail from the start. Consensus, known in Japanese as *nemawashi*, has not been created. Moreover, none of the participants have any incentive to help the experiment succeed. But most of all, there is simply not enough waste in the university hospital system to try and squeeze out increased productivity. In a year or two the government will announce that the DPC experiment has failed to meet its objectives and that will be the end of that. In the meantime, they at least can appear to everyone that they are doing something.

One last thought. The JMA has not opposed this DPC experiment. Does not that tell you something? Can you imagine an organization like the JMA giving up so easily if the outcome was not already preordained?

2. THIRD PARTY HEALTH INSURANCE

Supplementary health insurance has been available in Japan since the late 1980s. This insurance has traditionally been called cancer insurance. These indemnity-type policies are paid directly to patients in the case of a diagnosis of a disease or as daily remuneration in the case of hospitalization.

Until recently, the very idea of mixing private and public insurance was cause for shock to nearly everyone. Called *kongyo shingyo* (which can be translated as 'public and private healthcare insurance'), this practice was considered so shocking because of its implications that wealthy people can buy better health coverage and receive better care than other, less affluent Japanese citizens. In other words, *kongyo shingyo* appears élitist and undemocratic.

While *kongyo shingyo* has been a dirty term for a long time, it has recently emerged as a key issue in the healthcare debate. While traditionalists still find it distasteful, *kongyo shingyo* is gaining political support among some factions, especially the Ministry of Finance – which just happens to oversee the insurance industry and approves insurance policies under the auspices of the Financial Services Administration (FSA). It is noteworthy, too, that the MHLW officially opposes *kongyo shingyo*.

In the year 2000 – much to the chagrin of the MHLW and the JMA – SECOM, a security company that has taken indirect ownership of several Japanese hospitals, applied for and won approval for a policy that provides payments directly to hospitals at 1.5 times the normal reimbursement rate. This policy has stirred the pot because it implies that its policyholders would receive special treatment because of their higher reimbursement amounts. This 'élitist' idea, according to critics, flies in the face of fair and unbiased healthcare, which has long been the official, political and philosophical standpoint of Japan. This SECOM-initiated program has seen a strong backlash from both the MHLW and from the JMA. In response, SECOM seems to have curtailed its marketing and implementation of this program. Nonetheless, an important milestone was achieved – the birth of *kongyo shingyo*, which may have been all that SECOM wanted from the exercise in the first place.

PERSPECTIVE A:

MIXED PUBLIC/PRIVATE HEALTH INSURANCE IS THE PERSONIFICATION OF EVIL

The principle most basic to Japanese society is the ideal that all citizens are fundamentally equal, regardless of wealth or circumstance. Having said that, most people are not so naïve or idealistic as to believe that we live in a truly egalitarian society. Social inequality is a fact of life and there is no avoiding it. Despite these realities, however, it is essential that the basic services provided by the government to its population be fair and equal regardless of political, religious, or financial status. When a government stops striving for fairness, it loses its moral imperative and creates upheaval in the form of a widening rift between haves and have-nots.

As set forth in the constitution, healthcare in Japan is to be a fundamental and universal service mandated and administered by the government. As such, it is essential that a fair and equal system be maintained. Kongyo shingyo is the first step towards a two-tier system and a challenge to Japan's social ideals. The idea that the rich are eligible for levels of care beyond those available to the less affluent is contrary to the principle of Japan's social contract. Incursions against this contract and principle should not now or ever be tolerated under any circumstances whatsoever.

PERSPECTIVE B:

MIXED PUBLIC/PRIVATE HEALTH INSURANCE IS INEVITABLE AND POSITIVE

It is indisputable that humans are self-centered beings that choose their own interests over all others, including social equality. If a significant portion of the population has the means to pay for a level of care above and beyond that offered, a demand void will be created. Regardless of how the government responds, as demand grows, the unchallengeable economic principles of supply and demand will take over and the demand will be filled. Make no mistake: the demand will be filled.

As the problem of Japan's aging population grows, the increased rationing of healthcare services is inevitable. Decreasing services will result in lower standards of care and the population being deprived of new advances in medical science due to cost – even though the Japanese have the most savings of any country in the world. If the government does not provide a rational 'escape valve' for this building pressure to the existing system, a parallel healthcare system will almost certainly emerge – creating a true two-tier system completely separate from the social healthcare system. In fact, this is already happening. Some hospitals and clinics are operating completely outside the official system and are working on a fee schedule many times higher than that of the government's. One such upstart is the Sanno Hospital, a care facility that boasts a grand piano in its reception area, appointments for procedures, and – not surprisingly – a huge waiting list for patients seeking treatment. Treatment, it must be added, that will be paid for out of patients' own pockets.

Even mainstream hospitals are finding ways around onerous government rules that state that hospitals will forfeit all government reimbursements if they take any private patients outside the subscribed system. Working round the system is done in many ways. The most brazen offenders simply do it in the open while the slyer ones simply charge exorbitant room rates that offset the higher level of care. If the government is not careful, it will have a fully fledged shadow healthcare market on its hands – and one over which it will have no control.

Supporting *kongyo shingyo* is an honest way to confront the economic and societal realities facing the system. When these insurance products become widely available, risk-adverse Japanese citizens will snap them up – and, in doing so, also help the ailing insurance industry. *Kongyo shingyo* will also create a market for high technology drugs, devices, and other treatments that are simply outside the reach of the current cash-strapped system – again helping to boost the overall economy with more jobs and growth.

3. OUTCOME STUDIES

Many observers of the Japanese healthcare scene believe that arming consumers with information about the best hospitals and the best physicians would be a good way to assure quality through what essentially amounts to competition. Theoretically, those hospitals that can provide the best data would in turn get the most number of patients. There is little debate that the best possible way to rate a care provider is to chart their results in accordance with the quality of care they provide. In healthcare lingo, these results are called outcomes.

There has been a call by consumer groups, the press, and even – although less so – from some ministries to run outcome studies and make the results of these studies available to healthcare consumers. On the surface this appears to be a very logical way to proceed. Judge for yourself after examining the prevailing perspectives:

PERSPECTIVE A:

OUTCOME STUDIES ARE THE ONLY WAY OF PROVIDING VALUABLE DATA TO CONSUMERS

Consumers are hungry for real data, the kind they can use to make decisions about where to receive treatment. The Internet has made huge volumes of data available. The rumor mill is also constantly abuzz, humming about which doctor and facility is good and which bad. Through accreditation or certification, hospitals are now also working harder than they were to demonstrate to the public that they are performing quality medicine. But what does this all mean?

Even to those in the medical profession, it is hard to assimilate all this information and know where to go for top-quality medical care.

The only meaningful data understandable to everyone is raw, basic, data. Mortality. Morbidity. Length of stay. These areas would be a good start. Surly, now that we are in the highly-developed information age, this kind of data should be readily available.

Would it not be wonderful, for example, to be able to access a certain hospital's data and see that the survival rate is 88% for patients who underwent the same surgery that you need? And that the average length of time they spent in the hospital was six days? And that, when compared to the hospital average, your choice in hospitals and/or physicians are performing better on both counts by 22.6%? All of this is now possible. It is obvious why some hospitals would not want to share this information – especially those that fare poorly in comparative analyses. Such real market information for healthcare services is capable of creating a healthy climate of competition that is based on the only criteria that truly counts – outcomes and results.

I know that many people say that meaningful data cannot be provided because healthcare is too complex and that there are too many variables. Clearly, creating a system like the one described above would be complex and require a great deal of work. But with the computing power available today, surely it is possible. The real reason we lack an outcome-based system, one can argue, is because of resistance from those with vested interests, like the doctors and hospitals who would prefer – quite naturally – to work without clearly measurable accountability.

The only way to create a system that demonstrates real outcome evaluations is to have it come from the payer's side, whether it be government or private insurers. These are the only groups with the necessary mix of power, money and vested interests to develop and run such a system.

We need to create a method of gathering data so that we can correlate the outcomes of hospitals and individual physicians on a statistically relevant level. The technology exists. The consumer is hungry for this kind of data. We need to get beyond any silly ideas that creating this kind of database is too complicated. By identifying and rewarding good performers and penalizing bad ones, we will go a long way to fostering a true market environment in the healthcare field. And by doing, the patient, the system, and the payers will all win in the end.

PERSPECTIVE B:

OUTCOMES ARE SIMPLY INACCURATE, TOO DIFFICULT, AND – FOR THE MOST PART – WORTHLESS

It is not surprising that the average person would view outcome data as a panacea for healthcare problems. For someone who does not understand the complexity of biology, physiology, treatments, and pathology, it might seem a relatively easy task to rank both hospitals and physicians by the outcomes they produce. The problem is that it simply will not work.

The first thing that we need to understand is that hospitals and doctors don't typically cure patients. What we do instead is create an environment where the patient's own biological system can cure itself. The frustrating part about practicing medicine is that even textbook treatments sometimes result in poor outcomes. Conversely, there are situations where horrid treatment practice has resulted in an outstanding outcome. We all hope, of course, that statistically, good treatments result more often in good outcomes than the reverse, but we all need to understand that the most important part of determining a good outcome is the patient, not the doctor.

If you were running a hospital and wanted outstanding outcomes, it would be very easy to do: all you have to do is refer the most difficult cases elsewhere. These difficult cases are patients who are in the worst trouble and need the most help. Of course doing such a thing would be unethical, but it underlines the basic problem with outcome studies. Those physicians who are considered the best in their field generally get the most difficult cases and could very likely have worse statistical outcomes than those doctors with questionable skills who know their limitations and refer the tough cases elsewhere.

One opinion says that outcome studies should be used only with broad-based quality indicators, such as infection rates. Again, the problem is twofold. First, all a hospital needs to do to achieve low infection rates is constantly supply all their patients with antibiotics (already a common practice in Japan). Anyone willing to violate medical practice standards could achieve ideally low infection rates. On the other hand, a hospital that practices what is considered to be good medicine through the judicious use of antibiotics could lose a statistical competition to an inferior and less ethical hospital.

Easy solutions like outcomes seem fine until you really start analyzing the underlying issues. The only realistic standards that we can use to judge our healthcare providers are facility accreditation, professional education, and adherence to current practice guidelines. To try and do otherwise will only lead to a bureaucratic nightmare, with little practical benefits.

4. ADVERTISING

The issue of allowing doctors, hospitals, or clinics to advertise may seem like a minor one. In fact, however, it may well be one of the single most important healthcare-related issues of recent memory. There are several reasons why. First, if the government and other stakeholders agree to advertising, they are also in effect agreeing that a market dynamic does exist for healthcare, one that follows the basic economic principles of supply and demand. Second, the introduction of advertising refutes the standard line that all hospitals and care providers are equal. It also intensifies the competitive environment between hospitals and doctors which can promote higher quality.

Besides that mentioned above, the most important thing about medical advertising is that it has traditionally been solely in the government's domain. In fact, advertising is really the *only* tool that government has to manipulate the medical profession and their relationships with patients. Typically, the government creates new regulations to direct behavior in ways that it wants. But if the ban on advertising for medical institutions is lifted, the government has suddenly gone from creating regulations to relaxing them as a way of manipulating medical behavior.

The relaxing of advertising regulations has been at the heart of many government healthcare reform efforts. Here are some examples:

1) The empowerment of medical associations
2) Creating systems for certifying medical specialists
3) Creating requirements for Continuing Medical Education (CME)
4) Creating motivators for facility accreditation

There are several thousand professional medical associations, called *gakkai*, in Japan. *Gakkai* are large associations representing areas of medicine such as internal medicine, cancer, and the clinical laboratory. There are also associations specific to diseases such as cerebral palsy, rheumatoid arthritis, and the like. Many of these *gakkai* are regionally divided. Until recently, these *gakkai* were self-regulated study groups with various layers of organization. Some of the *gakkai* have created their own professional rules. The majority of them, however, consist of a relatively loose alliance of members and most commonly operate only with volunteers or a small administrative staff.

In 2004, things will change, however, because of new rules regulating advertising. The new regulations stipulate that in order for a physician to promote or advertise his specialty, he or she must be a member of a qualified *gakkai*. Criteria have also been created defining what comprises a qualified *gakkai*. Although these specific regulations are discussed elsewhere in this book, suffice it to say here that these new developments will empower *gakkai* beyond their wildest dreams since they will become the gatekeepers for medical advertising in Japan.

The use of *gakkai* to regulate advertising is merely the first step in how these associations could be used. This author believes that by using the politically acceptable platform of the *gakkai*, the government is setting the stage for the medical professional associations to take on other tasks such as providing credentials for medical specialties and the creation of disciplinary and review boards. Conduits for Continuing Medical Education (CME) requirements and even medical facility accreditation are other roles that the *gakkai* might one day be asked to fill. Although many of these changes seem unlikely to happen soon in the current political environment, advertising liberalization represents an important and manageable first step.

PERSPECTIVE A:

ALLOWING HOSPITALS TO ADVERTISE IS NATURAL AND WILL PROVIDE PATIENTS WITH USEFUL INFORMATION

There has always been advertising in Japanese medicine. The most powerful and most effective kind of advertising known to man: word of mouth. Word of mouth and reputation are why some hospitals, such as Tokyo University Hospital, Keio University Hospital, etc., are 'brands' that have effectively cornered the market in Japan. For the most part, reputations based only on school name are usually and essentially baseless and can actually do a tremendous disservice to patients seeking the best care.

Common sense says that not all doctors or hospitals have the same skills, knowledge, or facilities at their disposal. Allowing a hospital to advertise has numerous benefits. First, it gives patients information about a hospital's specialties so that they can choose the best one for their particular ailments. Second, it creates an incentive for hospitals to try and maintain the best science, facilities, and staff. Lastly, advertising allows the government to introduce a manageable amount of competition between hospitals.

The MHLW has ingeniously used the liberalization of advertising rules to try and improve the system. Even though advertising may be one of the only cards it can use in the face of the tremendous power wielded by the JMA, the ministry has played its hand brilliantly. Eventually, advertising will lead to patients choosing better physicians and facilities while driving them away from those facilities that fail to make the grade. This 'survival of the fittest' dynamic will leave both the patient and the healthcare system much better off.

The liberalization of advertising is not a panacea, of course. There will be problems with inaccurate information in ads. Also, will

Figure 25. Items that may be legally advertised (implemented April 1 2002)

Information regarding treatment content	• Accreditation of specialist doctors • Treatment methods • Number of operations • Number of deliveries • Average days spent in hospital • Number of patients by ailment
Information regarding facilities and personnel distribution	• The ratio of doctors and nurses compared to patients • Kiosk, cafeteria, childcare services, etc.
Information regarding the systems used by the medical institution	• Implementation of second opinion • Installation of electronic charts • Placement of patient counseling • Holding of case review commission • Introduction of in-patient treatment plans • Internal management system for medical safety
Evaluations of medical institutions	• Evaluation results from the Japan Council for Quality Health Care
Information regarding the management of medical institutions	• Occupancy rate of beds • Career summary of Chairman • External auditing • Evaluation of patient service system (ISO9000s)
Other	• Homepage address of medical institutions • The fact that it is one of the following medical institutions – Pollution-related medical institutions in the Pollution-Related Health Damage Compensation Law – Hospital for the emergency medical of children – Aids treatment hospital – Hospitals conducting research on the treatment of specified diseases, etc.

Source: 'The Survey on Actual Conditions Regarding Access to Japan Health Care Services,' July 2002, JETRO

patients be able to understand and use the information they are given effectively? While the argument in favor of advertising is compelling, it is also clear that rules need to be put in place to protect patients from false or misleading information.

PROSPECTIVE B:

ALLOWING HOSPITALS TO ADVERTISE CHEAPENS THE MEDICAL PROFESSION AND CREATES AN ENVIRONMENT FOR MISLEADING PATIENTS

It is sad to see the rules on advertising for medical facilities being relaxed. One reason for an overt, negative reaction to this liberalization is because of tradition. Many people believe that the medical profession stands above crass commercialization, and that advertising is really nothing more than bragging. Also, by advertising, what a doctor or hospital is essentially doing is telling patients that they are better than other hospitals or doctors. Are not doctors supposed to be colleagues, not enemies? There may well be a cultural element to these feelings, as well. Many Japanese people feel that humility is a virtue and advertising flies in the face of that and other traditional values.

There are other, more practical reasons, for the case against advertising. First of all, we have to remember that the practice of medicine is very complex and it is doubtful that most patients understand at any meaningful level the real merits of one hospital over another based on what gets put in their advertising. It is also likely that much of what gets advertised may even be misrepresented or glorified in some way to try and sway patients to one facility over another. The best advice to patients is to stay away from facilities or doctors who feel they must advertise. The facilities that do not have to stoop to this level probably already have plenty of patients, which should be proof enough of their competency.

The last point worth making about advertising concerns the underhanded way that the government is using it to manipulate the medical profession. Since people are competitive by nature, even honorable and traditional medical practitioners might get lured into unnatural, unnecessary competition because of the liberalization of the advertising rules. This transparent effort to force Japanese hospitals and doctors into accepting imported Western concepts such as CME and facility accreditation is a slap in the face to our medical system. Advertising should not be allowed under any circumstances in Japanese medicine.

5. PHYSICIAN LICENSING

Historically, and as in most countries, medical professionals in Japan are typically licensed for life once they have completed rigorous course work and passed their official examinations. While many countries have begun to change this practice by requiring ongoing competency evaluations, in Japan these professionals, whose ranks include doctors, remain licensed for life to practice medicine. While some moves have been made toward changing this system requiring regular examinations to ensure public safety, there is no actual legislation in the works to create a re-licensing requirement for physicians.

The one exception to this are recent rules in the area of physician specialists. In order to promote their specialty physicians need to belong to an accredited professional society. For this society to be accredited, it is mandatory for them to document the ongoing education of its members.

PERSPECTIVE A:

FOR THE GOOD OF PUBLIC SAFETY AND TO ENSURE BETTER MEDICAL CARE, PHYSICIANS SHOULD BE SUBJECT TO RE-LICENSURE

The public has a right to know that the professionals who care for them are competent, knowledgeable and up-to-date. If our society re-tests pilots and taxi drivers, why do we not regularly evaluate the physicians whom we entrust with our very health and life? The reasons can be traced to the Victorian notion that the medical profession is somehow above the scrutiny of mere mortals and that doctors are worthy of our blind trust. This concept is outdated in most industrialized countries which now require at least some level of oversight and competency evaluation. In Japan, however, the status quo remains unchanged and almost no physicians are evaluated or tested on a regular basis.

Under Japan's current system – or lack thereof – it is possible for a doctor to work for forty years and never once open a book or acquire new information of skills. It is equally conceivable that physicians operating their own hospitals could suffer from some mental or physical impairment which decreases their ability, or even makes them a danger to the public – and we would not even know it. Except for direct observations by helpless patients, there is no system in place to prevent these abuses to public trust from happening. These situations are indefensible in this day and age and must be rectified immediately.

The following actions must be taken:

1) All physicians should be required to take a regular examination every five to seven years.
2) The examination should cover recent topics in general medicine, including newly-available drugs and therapies as well as drug interactions.
3) A general evaluation of the mental state of the physician should be part of the exam and be designed to screen for dementia, mental disease, and/or drug and alcohol abuse.

It is clear that physicians and groups supporting physicians will oppose these proposals because, of course, they prefer to remain unchecked and unquestioned. But the world is changing and people are demanding and deserving of more transparency. The medical profession asks a great deal of trust of the public. It is about time medical professionals earned that trust and agreed to some levels of oversight and accountability.

PERSPECTIVE B:

THE RE-LICENSING OF PHYSICIANS IS A BAD IDEA. IT WILL PUT EVEN MORE STRESS ON THE SYSTEM AND INDIVIDUAL PROFESSIONALS WHILE NOT SIGNIFICANTLY INCREASING PUBLIC SAFETY

At a superficial level it is very difficult to argue with re-licensing requirements for physicians or other professionals. The fact is that, yes, there is a degree of incompetence and, in some cases, mental instability among the ranks of licensed doctors – just as with all sub-segments of any population. However, we all need to understand that being a doctor is a tough, demanding job.

After finishing medical school, all a doctor really has is a basic foundation of knowledge on which to build. From that time forward, physicians study and learn from every patient they see. The amount of learning gained from this kind of day-to-day work far surpasses any knowledge available in lectures and books. The constant influx of information gained from constantly interacting with human beings in real situations is invaluable, but it is a value very difficult to quantify through any kind of objective testing. The knowledge and experience gained through a physician's life is often more art than science.

Being a good physician involves constant decision-making. Making sound decisions requires a certain self-confidence, however, that some people unfortunately misinterpret as arrogance or over-confidence. The fact is that every doctor is constantly faced with extremely difficult questions. Some are value calls. Some questions have no right answers. Some questions they truly cannot answer and doctors may not know if they are doing the right thing or making the right diagnosis. These sorts of situations, typically, cannot be captured in books. Rather they come from a wealth and depth of experience that is nearly impossible to evaluate through any kind of standard examination.

If the government institutes re-licensing requirements for physicians, it is possible there may be some benefits. But, the negative aspects of such an idea must also be considered. We could lose many of our best practitioners because they refuse to subject themselves to such government-orchestrated humiliation. We may lose others with vast clinical experience simply because they have not kept up with some obscure technology or techniques that a test-maker deems important. We may also sacrifice the invaluable trust and confidence that patients place in their doctors.

Lastly, we must remember that a supervisory system is already in place in the form of professional societies. Doctors are also monitored by their peers and even by the patients who see them in action. These informal observers provide an effective observation system especially if mental or physical ailments are hampering performance.

There is no perfect person – nor perfect system. Mistakes will be made. Moreover, in an immensely complex field like medicine, differences of opinion will always exist. We need to trust medical schools to graduate physicians with the appropriate skills. We also need to trust that these people will learn and develop their skills throughout their careers. Lastly, we need to keep our own eyes open to watch for problem physicians and report any abuses. While some people may feel more confident if ongoing physician testing was implemented, the net positive effects would be negligible, and the negative impacts significant.

6. FACILITY ACCREDITATION

Until 1999 Japan had no viable system for accrediting its medical facilities. Before then, the only documentation necessary to open and operate a hospital was a valid physician's license – that never expires. A great deal has happened in the area of medical accreditation since then. The Japan Council of Quality Healthcare (JCQHC) was founded and a voluntary system of hospital accreditation was created. While getting off to a slow start, more than 1,000 of Japan's 9,000 hospitals are now accredited and the MHLW has just announced that there will be extra reimbursement points given to accredited hospitals. This bonus was also given to hospitals that have obtained ISO9001 accreditation. Such a move will likely increase the demand for this standard.

Accreditation of healthcare facilities has even extended to individual departments. ISO has recently adopted the ISO15189 standard for clinical laboratory medicine, for example, something that has also been embraced by the Japan Accreditation Board for Quality Assessment (JAB) as a Japanese standard. It is increasingly likely that ISO15189 will become the clinical laboratory standard for Japan in coming years.

This voluntary process of accreditation, backed by economic incentives in the form of increased reimbursements, is being applauded by patient groups and payers. But of course not everyone is happy.

Figure 26. Third party evaluation organizations

	Organization (System)	Method of application/ evaluation	Note
Third Party Evaluation of Medical Organizations	Japan Council for Quality Health Care (Hospital Functional Evaluation System)	• Hospitals that want to be evaluated make a request • Authorization and Evaluation is not related to the payments of Medical Care Security	• Since 1997 • As of June 17th 2002d, of approx. 9000 hospitals 695 had been evaluated
Third Party Evaluation of Long-Term Care Services	Elderly Service Providers Association (Silver Mark Accreditation System)	• Content and quality are evaluated for certain services • Application system	
	(It has been decided to introduce outside evaluation in long-term care services, and this will begin after the third quarter of 2002*1)		

Source: 'The Survey on Actual Conditions Regarding Access to Japan Health Care Services,' July 2002, JETRO

PERSPECTIVE A:

THE MEDICAL ACCREDITATION SYSTEM IN JAPAN IS NOT WORKING. IT ADDS COSTS AND FAILS AT ITS GOALS OF INCREASING QUALITY AND TRANSPARENCY

The JCQHC was a good idea implemented poorly. Its fundamental problem is that it is funded and run by the very professionals it claims to be overseeing. The organizers are the Japan Medical Association (JMA), the Japan Nursing Association (JNA), the Japan Hospital Association (JHA), and the Ministry of Health, Labour and Welfare (MHLW). The JCQHC was formed because these groups collectively feared that the MHLW would create its own independent inspection body.

The first problem with this new Japan hospital accreditation system is that it exists in a cultural environment not conducive to meaningful oversight and criticism. Inspections, for example, vary in severity depending on the political or social stature of a hospital and its leading doctors. Until inspectors start being totally candid about what they see in inspections, the value of this program is negligible.

The ISO inspection programs, most notably the ISO9001 and ISO14000 standards, may be an improvement in terms of their ability to cut through traditional barriers. However, the companies that administer these programs lack the necessary technical expertise to understand the complexities of many medical practices. In short, they can determine whether a particular document is there or not, but not if it is the correct document, let alone know if proper procedures are being followed. In saying this, however, having the ISO standard available is much better then giving the JCQHC a virtual monopoly on hospital accreditation – which would further corrupt the entire program.

Rather than something promoting quality, the new system has only created an extra administrative burden while adding costs to the system. The incremental value achieved from these programs is negligible.

Of course the current system is a great improvement over what we had in the past – nothing. But, further leaps are still needed to make the inspection system meaningful and worth the money. One way to meld the current constituents into a workable hospital accreditation system is for the JCQHC to become responsible for creating, improving, and maintaining the standard. It should then qualify and give deeming status to ISO certification bodies to coordinate and perform the actual inspections. There are over one hundred such companies in Japan – employing thousands of qualified inspectors – which have the horsepower to perform the inspections, the knowledge to perform a quality audit and, most importantly, are politically neutral. The JCQHC can also fill an advisory role by lending technical support during audits.

It is good that a system of hospital accreditation has arisen in Japan. It is unfortunate, however, that it is being operated by the very people it claims to oversee. The solution to this, as mentioned above, is to find a way of combining the advantages of the current commercial ISO accreditation companies with the JCQHC's technical expertise. The result would be a fairer and much more valuable medical accreditation system.

PERSPECTIVE B:

THE MOVES TOWARD ACCREDITATION ARE TO BE COMMENDED, PARTICULARLY IN TERMS OF INCREASING TRANSPARENCY AND RATIONALIZING HEALTHCARE IN JAPAN

Many of those involved in Japanese medicine have long felt that creating a valid medical accreditation system was not, given the current administration, politically feasible for a long time to come. The success of the JCQHC in such a short period is a testament to what Japan can do when it uncovers a problem and works hard to solve it. Lead by the JMA and the MHLW, the JCQHC researched other medical accreditation systems around the globe and created a useful and reasonable standard for Japanese hospitals. The JCQHC has also created a volunteer-based accreditation model based on proven formulas from the West.

In recent moves, the MHLW has announced that it will support the accreditation process by adding reimbursement incentives to JCQHC-accredited hospitals. The MHLW has also taken another positive step by allowing hospitals to advertise their accreditation status. In a spirit of fairness and balance, the MHLW also made ISO9001-certified hospitals eligible for increased reimbursement. The JCQHC itself, moreover, is in a constant cycle of self-improvement. It has moved away form the one-time inspection accreditation model to another that requires an inspection every five years, possibly moving to once every three years. Standards are becoming more rigorous every year, and another initiative under consideration is that of multiple accreditation levels which will clearly identify hospitals of superior quality. There is even talk about posting inspection results on the Internet to help patients evaluate hospitals.

In the specialty areas, Japan was quick to approve and is now implementing the ISO15189 standard for clinical laboratory medicine. Other specialty accreditation areas are likely to follow sooner rather than later. Japan has moved quickly and surely from being a country whose medical system was like a black hole to one whose system boasts increasing transparency and incentives for quality systems. This progress will ultimately increase efficiency and lower costs while at the same time improving the overall quality of patient care. The JCQHC should be publicly lauded for their role in this startling transformation.

7. CONTINUING MEDICAL EDUCATION

Mandating Continuing Medical Education (CME) for professionals who work in a constantly evolving field that is as technically complex as medicine seems obvious. In present-day Japan, however, there are no requirements for maintaining a medical license or for performing any procedure a physician deems fit. The only quasi-CME system in place is an evolving voluntary one coordinated by medical professional societies (*gakkai*). Increasingly, *gakkai* are demanding that their members get certain amounts of CME in order to claim or maintain membership – something they will need in order to advertise their specialty to prospective patients. Currently, credit for approved CME can be obtained in several ways. The most common of these is attendance at *gakkai* meetings or writing papers on relevant subjects.

While some progress has been made on the CME front, opponents argue that the current system is superficial and little real learning takes place. Proponents contend that the current system is adequate. While the truth likely lies somewhere between these perspectives, there is one irrefutable fact about CME: it offers a significant business opportunity. The creation and delivery of CME is a billion-dollar industry in both North America and Western Europe while in Japan it is virtually non-existent.

In other industrialized countries, CME is funded by pharmaceutical and medical device companies in the form of unrestricted educational grants. These companies are essentially obligated to sponsor such grants because it is to their benefit to do so. Physicians properly educated about new advances in medical science are more likely to recommend new products based on these scientific advancements. In the West, it is generally believed that this kind of education is significantly more effective at changing physician behavior than visits by medical reps.

No one can predict the future. But with CME, significant changes seem imminent and inevitable.

PERSPECTIVE A:

ADOPTING A WESTERN-STYLE INDUSTRY-FUNDED CME SYSTEM IS NOT SUITED TO JAPAN AND SHOULD BE AVOIDED

Profit-making companies should be excluded from CME just as they are from medical practice. Education needs to be administered by educators and clinicians based on professional responsibility, courtesy, and need that is not profit driven. To change this system would be tantamount to changing the code of honor of the medical community and would undercut the trusted place doctors occupy in our society.

How can we trust the motives of profit-motivated firms? We cannot. Why would they give money to create purely educational materials and learning environments? They would not. Clearly, profit is their only motive and they can only achieve their goals by manipulating the behavior of well-intentioned medical professionals. We simply cannot trust commercial enterprises to deliver accurate, unbiased educational materials or programs.

Companies that publish CME materials or administer CME programs are as suspicious as the firms that sponsor them. These companies are paid by pharmaceutical companies (or the like) to develop programs purely for the purpose of increasing the sales of whichever product has been targeted. Period. Such programs are nothing but blatant attempts at manipulating physician behavior and should not be allowed under any circumstances.

PERSPECTIVE B:

INDUSTRY-FUNDED CME PROGRAMS SERVE DOCTORS, THE SYSTEM, AND PATIENTS WELL. CME PROGRAMS ARE AN ADMIRABLE USE OF INDUSTRY FUNDS, PARTICULARLY WHEN COMPARED WITH TRADITIONAL PROMOTION METHODS

In an ideal world, all CME programs would be created and administered solely by academic organizations such as medical associations and universities. In that same ideal world, these programs would also be organized and administered by academic groups. Needless to say, our present world is far from ideal. Modern economic and practical realities dictate that many CME programs will either get funded and created by industry – or they will not get created at all.

The medical industry has the two vital components necessary to create CME programs. First they have the motive, which is simply to ensure that physicians understand new advances in medicine. The result of this education will be better, more modern patient care – and yes, in some cases, increased sales for some commercial enterprise or product. The second essential thing they have is the money to fund such programs. Medical associations do not have the cash for this purpose and neither does the government. The funding of CME is a win-win-win proposition. Patients win because their doctors are better equipped to diagnose and treat them. Doctors win because they get useful, high-quality educational materials at a reasonable price. And, medical companies win because they have a cost-effective and accountable way to educate their customers.

Some say that professional associations should administer their own educational programs. But, once again, the ideal must take a back seat to reality. Companies have the technical expertise, organizational ability, and budgets to create and administer such programs very effectively. The voluntary work forces of most professional associations do not. The simple answer is to establish some basic rules for administering accredited CME programs whether they are industry-sponsored or not:

1) All content must be authored by clinicians and academics of note in the relevant field.
2) All content must be reviewed and approved by the associated professional organization's education committee.

3) Materials and delivery systems should be evaluated by all physician participants.
4) Content should be reviewed and updated on a regular basis to maintain its status as official CME material.

If a proper monitoring system is instituted, the resources and motives of the medical industry and the sanctioning functions of professional associations could be combined to form an ideal partnership. Such a fusion is capable of quickly and efficiently creating a quality and accountable CME system in Japan in a way that no other partnership could.

8. HOSPITAL DEPARTMENT OUTSOURCING

Current regulations stipulate that all patient-centered hospital activities need to be done by hospital staff. Outsourcing of departments and procedures is limited to things such as janitorial and food service (with the exception of the clinical laboratory, which will be discussed later in this section). The practice of outsourcing a hospital department such as medical imaging or dialysis, for example, is not possible under the current rules. Western-style physician privileges, whereby doctors have the 'privilege' of working at certain hospitals while not employed by those hospitals, do not exist in Japan.

Recently there has been significant debate about allowing private corporations to contract with hospitals for selected patient services. Proponents of this plan say it would be very effective in areas with the following characteristics:

1) Lower patient risk
2) Repetitive procedures
3) Use of equipment and disposables

It is not surprising that the old guard remains firmly against the idea and very little deregulation has occurred in this area to date.

PROSPECTIVE A:

HOSPITAL SECTOR OUTSOURCING WILL INCREASE EFFICIENCIES AND QUALITY, AND IMPROVE THE ECONOMICS OF HEALTHCARE DELIVERY

It is hard to imagine a more complex organization than a hospital. In actuality, a hospital is more than just an organization; it is more like a collection of numerous organizations under a single roof. These mini-organizations (typically referred to as hospital departments) each have their own specific set of skills, utilize their own equipment and supplies, and are typically managed by a specialist. Examples of these departments are medical imaging, the clinical laboratory, rehabilitation medicine, dialysis, oncology, pharmacy, pediatrics, emergency medicine, etc.

Many hospital departments are responsible for performing repetitive tasks that lend themselves well to an assembly line type of operation. These kinds of departments use similar equipment and supplies and, as such, are prime candidates for outsourcing to large commercial types of organizations that can run the operations advantageously with their economies of scale. A management team can set up and oversee operating procedures in hundreds or even thousands of facilities, using a repetitive, mass- production approach. These organizations can bulk purchase or even manufacture their own materials at a fraction of normal cost. Besides their productivity advantages, commercial enterprise can innovate and find more effective methods of operations in ways that hospitals cannot. Perhaps most importantly, these facilities can compare the productivity, costs, and overall quality of one center against another, valuable data that can help weed out inefficiencies or incompetence.

Although there are numerous areas where the changeover to outsourcing is possible, interestingly, only one hospital department in Japan has been deregulated. For the last several years, large clinical reference labs have been contracting with hospitals to run their clinical laboratory and pathology services. It is unclear how and why this singular instance of outsourcing occurred since other hospital departments were not given this option. The absence of the JMA as a stakeholder in the field of clinical labs is the most likely reason, however.

Here is how clinical lab outsourcing works in Japan: the reference laboratory places and takes responsibility for all equipment, management, and personnel. The lab also bulk purchases equipment and supplies it to hospitals at prices some 50% to 80% lower than what single hospitals can get directly from equipment manufacturers. Furthermore, since as many samples as possible are sent to central testing facilities for processing in large batches, huge economic advantages are gained. While there are some complaints by medical technologists that they have lost control of their departments, quality levels seem more than adequate and grossly negligent laboratories either disappear or clean up their acts.

Other areas conducive to outsourcing include: dialysis, pharmacology, X-ray, Magnetic Resonance Imaging (MRI), mammography, dental services, audiology, optometry, rehabilitation medicine, and long-term care, among others.

If the areas mentioned above are deregulated, the overall management of hospitals will become much simpler as large, competent corporations take over many areas of patient services. Furthermore, such streamlining will allow physicians to focus on areas that require diagnostic judgment and complex decision-making. Also, the financial operations of a hospital would be equally simplified: hospitals will simply charge rent to outsourcing companies in exchange for referrals of a hospital's patients.

The outsourcing of hospital departments is an issue beyond healthcare and one relating to the country's total economy. If outsourcing is adopted, it would mean extremely promising business opportunities for both foreign and Japanese companies and entrepreneurs. Such an initiative would mean new jobs, an increase in the tax base, and would better justify the large investment Japanese society is making in healthcare for the elderly, since it would equally benefit the young by providing meaningful employment.

Laws limiting the ability of hospitals to outsource services should be withdrawn. Instead the government should promote the practice with tax incentives. Foreign companies that have the necessary know-how and technology should be encouraged to enter the Japanese market to offer these kinds of services.

PERSPECTIVE B:

ALLOWING PRIVATE COMPANIES TO TAKE OVER HOSPITAL SERVICES WILL HURT PATIENT CARE AND MAKE VITAL COMMUNICATION BETWEEN MEDICAL PROFESSIONALS DIFFICULT. FURTHER, IT WILL HARM THE ECONOMY BY DECREASING JOB AND BUSINESS OPPORTUNITIES

Allowing the cancer of profit-seeking businesses to invade the Japanese healthcare system is wrong and unthinkable. Department outsourcing is the first step towards the complete for-profit privatization of our precious system.

The concept of department outsourcing is fraught with problems. The most fundamental is that of communications. For hospitals to operate successfully – meaning for the benefit of patients – they must have constant, cooperative communication between medical professionals. This kind of communication is person to person and requires personal interaction in order to work, the kind that gets built up through years of working together. Having an outside company sending employees into a hospital will make this kind of relationship-building impossible. Because of hospital and non-hospital employees working together, factionalism will inevitably result and disputes will arise with no central authority to resolve them. In the end, this practice will lead first to a breakdown in communications and then to an irreparable tear in the fabric of the system. The most real and devastating impact will be on patient care.

The idea that outsourcing hospital departments will help the economy is preposterous. First of all, private companies will use automation whenever possible to limit personnel expenses and jobs will be lost. Unemployment will rise and the tax base will grow smaller. Also, medical suppliers will be forced to sell products at substantially lower prices due to bulk purchasing. As a result they will not be able to afford to offer hospitals higher service levels, which will decrease the number of employees again. The decreased revenues will accordingly affect the amount of money they can spend on research and development, limiting advances in patient care and again costing jobs.

The best example of this already failed practice is the outsourcing of lab services. Communication between professionals has already suffered. Turnaround time for samples has decreased, adversely affecting patient care. Diagnostic manufacturers are being forced to cut the size of their Japan operations due to the downward price spiral. If all that is not enough, loyal and conscientious employees have been forced out of work or made subservient to outside, profit-driven corporations.

At first glance, the idea of department outsourcing for hospitals may sound like a good one with its promise of increased productivity at lower cost. But if one has any true understanding about how hospitals and the people inside them work, the reality is very different. Clearly, department outsourcing challenges already overtaxed communication channels, creates factualism, increases medical errors, and hurts the entire economy with lower employment levels. This practice must be stopped.

9. NON-REIMBURSED HIGHLY ADVANCED MEDICAL TREATMENTS (HAMAT)

The Highly Advanced Medical Treatments, or HAMAT, program was developed in the late 1990s to accommodate technologies considered safe and efficient, but that were not to be included in the social health reimbursement scheme. At the time, the entire concept was revolutionary because it was in dramatic conflict with Japan's previous policy of equal and fair treatment for all members of society. While there are over one hundred technologies now included in this scheme, they have not gained wide acceptance.

Reasons for the relative lack of success of the HAMAT program to date are varied, but the following are some of the major causes:

1) Technology manufacturers see their products being included in HAMAT as a failure of their regulatory departments to have gained 'real' reimbursement from the national healthcare system. Because these technology producers feel that their products will never achieve mainstream use, they do not promote or educate the market on the advantages of using their products and technologies. Therefore, most physicians are never made aware of the existence of the new advances.
2) Physicians are conditioned to practice medicine using the prescriptive method with the reimbursement tables as their guidelines. For the majority of physicians, if a treatment is not reimbursed, it does not exist.
3) Even for physicians aware of the new technologies, most are reticent to ask patients to pay extra fees for a HAMAT procedure.
4) In many cases, the use of HAMAT requires that hospitals invest significant resources in equipment and training. Because of the likelihood of low use, few hospitals are willing to make this investment.
5) While several insurance companies have introduced supplemental healthcare policies that include some or all HAMAT procedures, it is not in their best interest to promote them. The tendency, therefore, is to use HAMAT as a marketing tool for attracting consumers to insurance products, but not to educate physicians

and hospitals on the availability of the policies and how to use them.

Regardless of the reasons, the HAMAT program has not been successful. Worse, there is no consensus about how to salvage the program and meet its original goals.

PERSPECTIVE A:

HAMAT IS A GRAVEYARD FOR NEW TECHNOLOGIES AND RUNS COUNTER TO QUALITY HEALTHCARE

To recognize that certain technologies are technically difficult or advanced enough to rate their own category is a good idea. Also, HAMAT's initial goals were good and honorable. But the Achilles heal of the system is the fact that these procedures have been excluded from the healthcare reimbursement system. Moreover, if the HAMAT system gained wide acceptance, it would lead to a two-tiered system, separating the Japanese population into haves and have-nots. This division is simply not acceptable in Japan's social framework.

Since the HAMAT system already exists, there is no turning back. It will not be supported, however, by hospitals, physicians, or the relevant technology manufacturers. HAMAT is now used by MHLW bureaucrats as a catchall for technologies deemed inappropriate for Japan for either practical or fiscal reasons. Politically, regulatory approvals are still also necessary. As long as HAMAT remains in this moribund state, there should be no excessive harm to the system. But, if HAMAT's technologies begin to enjoy a wider acceptance, the resulting destabilization caused by the rupture of Japan's social contract (not to mention the constitution) relating to the universal right of fair and equal healthcare will be devastating.

Several factors will continue to ensure that HAMAT is unsuccessful. First, it is very difficult for manufactures to justify significant promotional expenses for a products classified as HAMAT. Second, it is nearly impossible for hospitals to justify the cost for adopting new technology. Finally, because of the first two factors, there will continue to be a general lack of awareness by both physicians and patients.

HAMAT is a graveyard for technologies. This system can be maintained for political expedience. But technologies that promise real value for patient care should be added to the national reimbursement system and set at appropriate reimbursement levels.

PERSPECTIVE B:

HAMAT CAN BE VALUABLE TO ALL STAKEHOLDERS IF WE CAN CHANGE THE TOTAL RELIANCE ON THE NATIONAL HEALTHCARE REIMBURSEMENT SYSTEM

The reality of the situation in Japan is clear. The system is being scissored by the combined forces of budget constraints and the increased cost of advancing medical technologies. One option for the healthcare system is to ignore these new technologies to the detriment of the patient in favor of saving public funds. However, in our current information age, the public will increasingly demand access to these life-saving measures.

If the public purse is closed to these types of technologies and the public insists on their inclusion, the only rational answer is to introduce a system that allows patients access by choice and at an extra cost. This was and remains the goal of the HAMAT program.

Unfortunately, the major stakeholders have shunned HAMAT and have forced it into relative obscurity. Distasteful as it may be, the reticence on the part of the heavily indoctrinated socialist physicians and government bureaucrats is not surprising. As for the medical product manufacturers who have joined the conspiracy against this potentially useful program, however, we can only feel disgust.

The reason for this lack of corporate support is clear. Companies have been spoiled by the easy earnings of a cozy government reimbursement scheme. To market a HAMAT product takes more work and, initially, involves more risk than with products automatically reimbursed by the government. By consensus, trade organizations like the American Chamber of Commerce have chosen to ignore the opportunities that HAMAT could provide, choosing instead to rely only on the opportunities that government reimbursement programs provide.

The cold, hard truth is that HAMAT represents a wonderful opportunity for the medical industry, but only if lead by the corporate healthcare establishment. The following is a formula, championed by medical product manufacturers, that could ensure HAMAT's success by creating a lucrative market-place for these new technologies:

1) Manufacturers and supplementary healthcare insurers need to meet and collaborate. This collaboration would consist of an exchange of data so that insurance companies could create

precise actuarial tables for these technologies as they become increasingly widespread.

2) Companies should embrace the free-market dynamics that HAMAT provides for. Within the HAMAT system, there is no restriction on pricing or marketing, because it is all private pay. Those companies with good technologies offering real value could compete in the market-place openly and freely.
3) Of course the companies that choose to market their products using the HAMAT classification would face certain challenges. These challenges include educating hospitals and selling them on the idea and value of adopting the relatively expensive HAMAT technologies. It would also involve educating doctors on the use of the new methods. But, with skilled salesmanship and an increasing number of potential patients with supplementary healthcare insurance, medical product companies are likely up to the task – if they choose to do so.

HAMAT represents the single largest opportunity for medical manufactures today as well as the only plausible route for offering these technologies to Japanese patients under the public sector's current financial constraints. The insurance, medical equipment, and pharmaceutical industries should collaborate and implement a staged strategy for utilizing HAMAT. Although such a plan will surely take time, it will just as surely be more beneficial than the alternative of waiting for a resourceless government to take action.

10. SPECIALLY DESIGNATED HIGHLY ADVANCED HOSPITALS

In close association with the government's HAMAT (Highly Advanced Medical Treatments) program, a new classification of hospitals was launched in the mid 1990s. Until that time, any hospital could perform any procedure it wished. Highly Advanced Treatments were part of this mix and institutions were motivated to do them because of their relatively high reimbursement rates. The MHLW initially designated 273 hospitals as Highly Advanced, and hence granted them special status as well as giving them a monopoly on these leading-edge treatments. It was generally felt that the right to perform these potentially profitable procedures would be a good incentive for designated hospitals to upgrade their facilities to meet HAMAT's procedural requirements.

The ability to brand and differentiate themselves did act as an effective driver for hospitals to participate in this program. The profit aspect of performing these kinds of procedures was much less successful, however, and there is more than one reason for the profitability shortfall. The key factors are the lack of third-party payers and the risk-adverse nature of hospital administrations that did not want to make necessary investments. That hospitals did not want to take risks should not come as a surprise – for nearly fifty years they have been working under a reimbursement scheme that essentially guaranteed them profit.

The main criticism of the program was the way hospitals were designated as highly advanced. At the time the program was initiated, not even the JCQHC was operational and there was essentially no effective referee to make these decisions rationally, transparently, and effectively. By default, the system had to fall back on the 'good ole boy' system that promoted as Highly Advanced those hospitals in good political standing – without any other meaningful criteria. This criticism has lessened in recent years thanks to the increased acceptance of the JCQHC and other healthcare reform measures.

The function and role of the specially designated Highly Advanced Hospital program is evolving. This designation now can be used as an effective marketing tool. It may also bring higher earning potential in a DRG prospective-type payment environment, not to mention the new reimbursements available to JCQHC accredited facilities.

PERSPECTIVE A:

THE HIGHLY ADVANCED HOSPITAL PROGRAM SHOULD BE EXPANDED

One of the major problems facing Japan's healthcare system is the proliferation of the same procedures in too many facilities. Concentrating difficult and/or expensive procedures in a small number of centers can be highly effective in increasing efficiencies and lowering costs – but this is not what's happened. The Highly Advanced Hospital programs should be expanded in accordance with specific criteria. Criteria should be procedure-specific and take into account general hospital standards as well as specialty criteria.

In the area of general overall hospital criteria, the successful maintenance of JCQHC and/or ISO9001 accreditation should be included. Specific requirements need to be established in the areas of certified specialists, minimum facility requirements, as well as the minimum number of procedures done per year and per each practicing clinician.

If the criteria mentioned above are incorporated, this program should be expanded to include any hospital that wishes to submit to the qualification process. Of course, it is also important to offer adequate incentives. Obviously there will be financial incentives commensurate with the increased patient load. But additional incentives such as increased reimbursement rates should also be considered.

The Highly Advanced Hospital Program has evolved and matured. The fundamental premise of the program was well-founded and the program now enjoys even better prospects for meaningful growth through the expansion of the program to any facility that meets the overall and specialty requirements.

PERSPECTIVE B:

THE HIGHLY ADVANCED HOSPITAL PROGRAM SHOULD BE ABANDONED THEN COMPLETELY REWORKED

The concept behind a system that allows only hospitals that have demonstrated proficiency in certain procedures to perform them is simply common sense. That Japan has allowed any hospital or any doctor to perform any procedure for so long is an abomination. The Highly Advanced Hospital Program was launched with good intentions, to be sure. But, it was launched at a time when Japan's 'good ole boy' system ruled the day and, as a result, a large number of hospitals were accepted into this program for the wrong reasons: political ones. No objective criteria were used in making selections.

Times have changed and hospitals enrolling in the program of late are subject to increased scrutiny. The old guard remains entrenched, however, and still holds all the trump cards. Until this elite group meets the same standards as the newer entrants, the entire program will remain corrupt and less than ideal. The only way to create meaningful change that meets the goals of the Highly Advanced Hospital programs is to start over.

Clear and transparent criteria must be written in stone. These should include requirements for accredited specialists (for whatever specialty applies) as well as regulations defining the minimum number of procedures that must be performed by specialists each year to ensure that they maintain competency.

Some may argue that the reform of the current system would be the most expedient and efficient way of rectifying problems. The drawback to this approach is that it doesn't deal with the central problem and remove the underlying rot built into the foundation of the program. All hospitals, regardless of their pedigree, must be held to uniform standards. The only way to achieve the results we need is starting over.

11. CREDENTIALED HOSPITAL ADMINISTRATORS

Hospitals are complex organizations filled with people doing a variety of jobs. Managing these organizations requires skill in administration, finance, personnel, inventory control, information technology, risk management, public relations, and even marketing. Moreover, every one of these areas is affected by the inherent complexity of medical science. According to Japanese law, all private hospitals must be owned and operated by doctors. Lately, there are some opinions suggesting that professional managers with the appropriate skills and education would be more effective at operating hospitals than doctors whose skills are more science- and medicine-based.

There are a number of challenges to overcome if professional hospital administrators are to become players on the Japanese healthcare stage. First, hospital administrator courses would need to be instituted at the university level as a distinct discipline. While it may be possible to offer such a degree solely to licensed physicians, it may also be practical to invite non-physicians as well into such a program. In fact, steps are being taken in this direction. Koichi Kawabuchi, for example, is focusing on healthcare, and has received funding to start a hospital administration course at prestigious Hitotsubashi University. It is yet unclear if these programs will receive support from the Ministry of Education or, perhaps more importantly, from the MHLW. But, many insiders hope Kawabuchi succeeds.

The biggest obstacle to such a plan is the attitude of doctors and the JMA. This is an emotionally charged subject from whichever perspective you choose.

PERSPECTIVE A:

HOSPITAL OPERATORS MUST BE DOCTORS. HOSPITALS ARE NOT FACTORIES AND THEY CANNOT BE RUN AS SUCH

It is easy to see why ordinary people would suggest that business types should run hospitals. Business people could operate hospitals as they do factories with the patients replacing widgets as products. The increased business acumen of professional managers would mean more patients processed cheaper and faster. These managers could even find ways to automate processes currently done by people. In time, perhaps, we may even have hospitals resembling the great robotic factories of the automobile industry. Now think: is this what you want medicine to become?

While some of the ideas above may be exaggerated, they clearly represent the reasons why doctors should remain in control of hospitals. Hospitals fill a very special role in our society: to treat our fellow human beings in their most serious times of need. Hospitals deal with life and death – and the accompanying emotions of people when they are most vulnerable. You cannot learn the role that hospitals fulfill in our society through business or even from medical books. The only way to learn and understand the realities of hospitals is by interacting with and treating thousands of patients. From the perspective of patients or their loved ones, it is clear that hospitals run by accountants or business executives is a terrifying idea.

It has been suggested that perhaps hospital administration should become a new academic discipline leading to a degree. To satisfy concerns that students of this new faculty may not be knowledgeable about the science of medicine, it has also been suggested that perhaps only licensed doctors should be admitted into such programs. Over time, it may actually become law that only these specially trained physicians can run hospitals. A future where only specially trained hospital administrators can run hospitals is only marginally better than hospitals being managed by professional business people. By necessity, business-specialist doctors will become distanced from the needs of patients. They will be taught to look at spreadsheets and productivity reports, not patient charts. Over time, the medical license on the wall will represent only a distant memory.

Doctors may not make the best business people. Perhaps hospitals can be run more efficiently by trained business executives. But, if so, what are the costs in terms of dehumanization? What human needs will be sacrificed for the sake of productivity? To think that hospitals can be run the same way as businesses is ludicrous. Anyone with such an idea should be kept as far away from hospitals as possible.

PERSPECTIVE B:

HOSPITALS ARE VERY COMPLEX PLACES AND GROW MORE SO EVERY DAY. RELAXING THE RULES ABOUT HOSPITAL MANAGEMENT WILL GREATLY INCREASE EFFICIENCY, LOWER COSTS, AND LOWER RISKS

Whether it is an academic organization, a for-profit business, or a healthcare facility, every organization has special needs. The idea that we train people to be teachers or business executives but don't require or even provide for specialized training for hospital administrators is foolhardy.

The only reason that doctors run hospitals in Japan is historical; hospitals were originally just the offshoot of clinics that had been set up by physicians. As these facilities grew and became more complex, the physician-administered hospitals became powerful and influential, which translated into wealth. The JMA opposes the idea of professional hospital administrators not for patient compassion issues; they do so purely because they don't want to share their wealth and power.

Having a foundation in medical science is clearly an important asset for administering a hospital. At the same time, this job requires skills that are not taught in medical school. Like it or not, a hospital is a business. And for the hospital business to be run efficiently and competitively, business skills and knowledge are required.

Under the new prospective payment (DPC) system, hospitals will be forced to face the harsh realities of the business world. Hospitals that operate efficiently, with high levels of patient satisfaction and superior financial performances will flourish. Hospitals that fail to measure up will go under. It follows, then, that hospitals with professional management will succeed in this contest and – make no mistake – this is a contest involving the survival of the fittest. The problem, once again, is political. Due to pressure from entrenched stakeholders, Japan's universities still have not created accredited courses or a credential system for hospital administrators. The creation of such a system is the first and most fundamental step that needs to occur. Of course, as motivation for qualified people to take these courses, the requirement that hospitals could only hire certified hospital administrators would be ideal. A compromise position might be that such a requirement would initially only be for government hospitals. Another concession might be that the professional administrator report initially to the physician in charge.

A system of training, credentialing, and mandating the use of hospital administrators will become increasingly important with the advent of prospective payment systems. In fact, it could be the single most important factor in the successful implementation of DPC in general and to the survival of individual hospitals in this new and changing environment.

12. STANDARDIZED CRITICAL PATHWAY REGIMES

Throughout the healthcare system, clients, clinicians, and healthcare administrators are searching for ways to further increase the systemization of healthcare practices. Given the advances in computing power, it should be possible to assemble and store statistically significant data that catalogs the outcomes for different disease states in relation to the various treatment methods available. After such data becomes organized and coherent, it should be possible to create disease-specific critical pathways. This creation of critical pathways is seen by some as a rational way of systematizing some key areas in the healthcare system.

The MHLW has seen the development of critical pathways as a key element in administrating the prospective payment (DPC) system. If critical pathways were developed, proponents claim, they would offer higher quality and predictability when compared to the current 'a la carte' method of deciding treatments. In fact, significant work has already been done with especially chronic conditions, such as diabetes, where the number of patients is high and the progression of the disease relatively predictable.

The idea of critical pathways also relates closely to the development of formularies, which are lists of drugs or collections of recipes, formulas, and prescriptions for the compounding of medicinal preparations. For manufacturers, gaining access to these formularies is invaluable for gaining market acceptance and the utilization of products and procedures.

PERSPECTIVE A:

CRITICAL PATHWAYS MAY HAVE LIMITED APPLICATION BUT, FOR THE MOST PART, THEY SIMPLY DO NOT WORK. INSTEAD THEY CREATE A BUREAUCRATIC MAZE AND STIFLE CREATIVITY AND INNOVATION

There are several major problems relating to the creation and implementation of critical pathways. First and foremost is the number of variables. They are simply so numerous that it is very difficult to assemble meaningful data. Each patient has unique characteristics. Clinicians typically need to deal with multiple conditions and lifestyle issues, not to mention psychological elements. As with any data entry and utility, garbage-in equals garbage-out. Accuracy and consistency when entering data for even the baseline condition of a patient will result in gross irregularities. The current available technology simply cannot accommodate such complexities. Critical pathway analysis may work in some cases but may fail miserably in others.

The main reason that these kinds of programs are being pursued is because the government wants to exercise control over physician judgment and therapeutic decision-making, as it already does through the current fee-for-service reimbursement point system. Considering the costs involved, however, it is not surprising that government wants this element of control. The problem here is that a massive and costly bureaucracy is needed to exercise this level of control. Physicians and administrators will end up spending more time on paperwork than on diagnosing and treating patients.

As you have heard time and again, the practice of medicine is as much art as it is science. Physicians who don't practice their skills constantly lose their ability to follow their instincts. If the practice of medicine is reduced to following formularies, medicine will suffer. Doctors will become complacent and there will be little innovation or discovery of new methods or techniques. The randomness introduced by skilled people with the ability to exercise judgment is one of the most important factors for learning and advancing new practices in medical science.

Critical pathways are an interesting concept that may be of some use in the future. Current technology, however, is still too immature to accommodate the complexity that is human illness. Critical paths will also result in the creation of massive and costly bureaucracies and will impede creativity and innovation.

PERSPECTIVE B:

CRITICAL PATHWAYS, ONCE DEVELOPED AND REFINED, WILL BECOME A KEY TOOL FOR HOSPITALS. THEY WILL TAKE THE GUESSWORK OUT OF MANY DISEASE TREATMENTS, PROVIDE CONSISTENCY AND ULTIMATELY SAVE MONEY

The most difficult part of practicing medicine is diagnosing disease. Many attempts have been made to try and create diagnostic computer programs, but to very little positive effect. Unquestionably, the diagnosis of disease needs to be performed by humans. However, once a definitive diagnosis has been made, the treatment options are often limited and, in some cases, this aspect of care is already standardized in many ways. Creating critical path guidelines based on a definitive diagnosis is possible with currently available technologies. It is also prudent, given the current finances of the healthcare system.

The development and implementation of critical pathways are especially important as we move from the current fee-for-service system towards a prospective payment one. Physicians can use their diagnostic skills and, once a definitive diagnosis is made, they can rely on critical pathways for guidance. Of course, any system requires flexibility to handle special patient conditions and circumstances and this flexibility should be incorporated into any critical pathways system.

Another key advantage to the critical pathway system is the ability to evaluate and reward quality innovations and technologies transparently and openly. Manufacturers can demonstrate how their technologies can enhance critical paths and gain approval for their use in whatever particular formulary applies.

Once critical pathways are developed, the system will benefit from increased productivity and lower overall costs. Physicians will become accustomed to the standardized treatment regimes that rely on their diagnostic skills. The repetitive aspect of the pathway approach will also allow healthcare teams to become well practiced and more efficient. This system will also allow hospitals, hospital systems, and even the central government to save money by making bulk purchases of products designated in formularies. The purchase of these products will become increasingly predictable.

Despite what critics claim, critical pathway programs can be implemented and offer many advantages. They need to be implemented slowly and deliberately, of course, but hospitals moving from fee-for-service to a prospective payment system will gain in any number of ways.

13. NUMERICAL MINIMUM PROCEDURE REQUIREMENTS

Some Japanese healthcare critics contend that there is a problem with some hospitals performing only small numbers of certain kinds of procedures. Unless a procedure is done often, it is argued, productivity is low and the performing doctor's proficiency is questionable. A proposal designed to deter this practice is gaining momentum. This plan would mean lower reimbursement rates for hospitals that fail to reach numerical benchmarks.

Low-volume procedures happen because hospitals are after the higher reimbursement rates available for those procedures that pay more than routine treatments. Thus, the argument goes, decreasing reimbursement levels will eliminate this less than ideal practice.

Smaller hospitals, of course, object to this proposal since they cannot compete with larger institutions, volume-wise. As a way of combating this criticism, backers of the new proposal have suggested that the minimum number requirement be extended to include individual doctors and not just facilities.

PERSPECTIVE A:

NUMERICAL MINIMUM PROCEDURE REQUIREMENTS ARE IRRATIONAL AND SHOULD NOT EVEN BE CONTEMPLATED

Physicians – not government bureaucrats – have the right to choose what procedures they perform. Doctors and hospitals are under enough pressure and don't need yet another big brother spying on their every move. Introducing minimum procedure requirements will simply mean more bureaucracy in a system already hobbled by red tape. While there are, admittedly, certain procedures that should only be performed by practiced experts, responsibility for referral and referral location should and must lie with primary care physicians. In some cases, referrals may go to an equally small hospital that has demonstrated expertise in a particular area. In other words, size doesn't matter. Talent does.

Moreover, it is wrong to assume that larger hospitals deliver better care and are more efficient than smaller facilities. In fact, the opposite is often true. Large hospitals deal with thousands of patients and are therefore less personal. Although larger facilities may have fancier equipment, they consistently fail to provide the kind of close attention to patients that smaller facilities do.

There is no question that abuses of the system occur. Some unscrupulous doctors may well perform procedures that they aren't qualified for or practiced at. But, it is important to realize that these kinds of doctors work in large and small hospitals alike and some may perform lots of procedures while others may do only a few. The only way to stop abuses in the system is to go after the abusers themselves. A blanket policy is simply overkill that penalizes good doctors and – more importantly – needy patients.

PERSPECTIVE B:

NUMERICAL MINIMUM PROCEDURE REQUIREMENTS SHOULD APPLY BOTH TO HOSPITALS AND TO INDIVIDUAL PHYSICIANS

Japan does more advanced procedures in more hospitals than anywhere else in the world. These high numbers reflect the fact that a large number of Japanese doctors perform very few procedures, particularly when compared to their colleagues in other industrialized nations where certain doctors specialize in certain kinds of operations. Common sense dictates that facilities that do more of these kind of procedures are better, more proficient and more productive than those that don't. In other words, practice makes perfect.

Why do some doctors choose to do only a small number of procedures? In some cases the reason is the rural setting where the patient is too ill or too old to travel. It could also be that certain patients trust certain doctors and want their procedure done by someone they know. There may also, however, be another, less noble motive. Hospitals are facing tough financial times. Many of the procedures in question are highly reimbursed. Putting two and two together, we must question if some procedures are done simply for financial reasons.

If malpractice litigation was a viable option in Japan, the need for a government system mandating minimum requirements may not be necessary. But, without such a balancing force, implementing numerical requirements is the only rational alternative. First and foremost, patients are typically not served well in low-use environments. While no statistics are available, it is easy to envision increased morbidity and mortality in situations where practitioners are inexperienced. Second, the system simply cannot afford the decreased productivity associated with servicing highly dispersed care environments. It is just too expensive.

A system mandating that both physicians and hospitals need to perform a minimum number of procedures in order to qualify for reimbursement needs to be established immediately. Some exceptions could be made for rural hospitals and for intern residency programs. Because of the bureaucracy already in place, collecting and monitoring such data should not be overly onerous. Enforcement should also be viable.

Adopting numerical minimum procedure requirements would force smaller hospitals to specialize in specific areas. They would also increase referrals. Thus, facilities with higher competency levels would do more procedures. The result will be higher quality for less cost.

8 Immigration

Historically, Japan has been called by some an insular country with restrictive immigration policies. This tendency, along with the aging of the population and low birth rates, have all been contributing factors in the healthcare crunch that Japan now faces. Of all these factors, however, some observers suggest that the only controllable variable among them is immigration policy. A less restrictive immigration policy, it has been argued, could bring more younger people to Japan and lessen the burden on the youth and young adults who face a future of overwhelming financial and social responsibility.

PERSPECTIVE A:

IMMIGRATION WILL CAUSE MORE PROBLEMS THAN IT WILL SOLVE

We have seen the power and benefits that immigration has brought to countries like the United States, where each wave of new blood has brought vitality and the will to succeed under any circumstances. It is now being proposed by some that Japan adopt a more open immigration policy as a way to counterbalance the continued graying of Japanese society. Some of the more radical views, in fact, suggest that a new immigration policy should have Japan openly recruiting immigrants. As anyone who understands Japan can tell you, this is an idea fraught with problems and will not serve the greater good.

There are fundamental problems with this idea. Japan is one of the most densely populated countries in the world. As a result, the success that Japan has had in the past, and on which all future success must be based, results from the close-knit social unity that binds all Japanese. This societal characteristic is certainly is not unique to Japan, but Japan's lack of usable land and large population make it more necessary than in other nations. Infusing Japan with large numbers of people who do not share a common social contract and have differing cultural norms and languages will cause untold problems.

Although it could be argued that many people share the idea that Japan is a society unsuited for an influx of new immigrants, this viewpoint is rarely discussed openly because people are afraid of being labeled as bigoted or xenophobic. It must be emphasized, however, that such an attitude is not prejudice at all. Instead, it is simply a very practical and realistic assessment of the situation. If immigration is allowed at all, it should be slow and well managed so that the entrants are given the time and means to assimilate into the Japanese culture and language as smoothly and successfully as possible.

PERSPECTIVE B:

IMMIGRATION IS THE ONLY PRACTICAL SOLUTION TO JAPAN'S AGING PROBLEM

Clearly, the idea of flooding Japan with a wave of immigrants does not sit well with many, if not most, Japanese who are – generally speaking – most comfortable when surrounded by others who have a the same culture, values, and language. While it may not be politically correct to say so, frankly, most cultures and most people are probably the same in this regard. Having said that, however, Japan is in a real bind and some kind of solution must be found. After all, what are the available options? Force women to have more babies? Create a scheme whereby people will die quicker? Realistically, the only route open to Japan is to invite other people to come and live in Japan, decreasing the average age of the population and attempting to reap any benefits that the new citizens would bring with them.

At present, Japan is in a promising position to attract well-educated people from a good number of Asian countries. For many people in these countries, a move to Japan would represent new economic opportunities presently unavailable to them in their own lands. If Japan handled such a campaign properly, it should be able to attract highly educated people who share, for the most part, a not too dissimilar racial and cultural background. In fact, Japan has the perfect vehicle for attracting promising youth from overseas in the form of its increasingly underutilized university system. Even language issues could be overcome with young energetic people coming to Japan to study and perhaps stay permanently.

A significant number of young productive workers would do wonders for Japan's tax base, as well as bring forth a new era of innovation and creativity. This opportunity, however, will not last forever. As other Asian economies get stronger, and Japan's potentially weaker as the graying of society continues, the incentive to immigrate to Japan will decrease dramatically.

To conclude, Japan has serious demographic problems that need to be solved and immigration is one way to do so.

9 Conclusions and Recommendations

Contrary to my initial plan, my editor and several contributors have convinced me that this work would be incomplete without a conclusion or a summary of my views. I hesitated to do so because during the past fifteen years of working in and studying many areas of Japanese healthcare, I know how complex the issues are, and how easy it is to oversimplify in an attempt to draw conclusions. Given that, let me try and summarize my views and ideas in a manner in which I am comfortable.

First and foremost, it needs to be stressed that the nature of the problems facing Japan is not particularly unique. What *is* unique is the timing of these problems: the demographic tidal wave of a rapidly aging population confronting universal medical coverage at a time when the economy is least able to handle it. For other countries facing similar futures, Japan will be an intriguing test case with huge ramifications.

I believe that most insiders basically understand what changes need to happen in the healthcare sector. The most basic of these changes relate to the fundamental drivers of care delivery, including:

a) Insuring that healthcare professionals are appropriately trained
b) Rational economic foundations are put in place
c) Universal standards and protocols are defined and enforced

While most insiders may agree that the aforementioned goals represent 'true north,' or the proper direction in which to go, few can agree on to how to get there. As with most human endeavors involving large numbers of people (and large amounts of money) there is an overwhelming political element to overcome. For better or worse, those in the political driver's seat will always determine the direction of the system. There's one powerful force, however, that can undermine even the strongest political will and position: economic reality.

The political constituents in Japan consist of the Japan Medical Association, government bureaucrats (including those at the MHLW and METI), patient groups and companies representing the medical industry. In my judgment, some of these constituencies are over-represented and some are under-represented. Herein – above all other considerations – lies both the problem and the potential solution. The only way to reach 'true north' is through an improved balance between these constituencies.

The current political balance is greatly weighted towards the JMA, which is supported to a large degree by the MHLW. While METI does have some counterbalancing effect because of its sway over economic matters, patient groups and the medical industry are significantly under-represented. The result of this political mix is a precarious coalition that supports socialist policies over more capitalist ones. Another characteristic of the current rule is a lack of transparency and accountability, particularly in relation to doctor-patient relationships. Lastly, this political balance under-utilizes medical technologies and medicines which could provide greater efficiencies and better patient care.

In saying all this, it is important to note that there have been great strides made in the past 10 years. I can clearly recall being called 'dim-witted' in the early 1990s when I predicted the changes to come in Japanese healthcare. 'They won't happen in your lifetime,' I was often told. At the risk of self-aggrandizement, I can report that – on most counts – history has proven me right and great strides have been taken toward rationalizing and improving both care delivery and the financing of the system. There is now a system of hospital accreditation that, while offering admittedly low levels of transparency, is still a huge improvement over the situation in the past. At least in government-funded hospitals, chart information is now available to patients. A prospective payment system is going into effect in university hospitals, reversing the inverse economic incentives of the fee-for-service system. These are only some of the changes that have occurred – and most of them in the last several years. But once again we can't forget politics. All of the changes mentioned above have occurred because of subtle shifts in the political winds that are moving away from the physician and towards the patient.

Unfortunately, this power shift is not due to some massive new awareness. Instead, it is occurring because of the new economic realities associated with Japan's economic doldrums and its aging population. I predict that this trend will continue and even intensify to the point that the political pendulum could very well swing over in the other direction – even past the ideal line that we have termed 'true north.' It is possible that Japan's socialistic healthcare system could become almost rabidly capitalistic. As older, wealthier patients demand better care and the system cannot afford to pay for it, a parallel system of payers and providers could emerge to satisfy this demand. The result would be healthcare in two tiers, one for the rich and the other for everyone else. Such a change will likely complicate rather than improve healthcare delivery.

While these future issues make for interesting conversation, the real questions concern the next half-decade. Against my better judgment, here are my predictions about what will happen to Japanese healthcare over the next five years:

1) Although university hospitals will impede its implementation, the prospective payment (DPC) system will eventually be adopted and expanded throughout the healthcare system. Physician fees will be excluded from the formularies.
2) The government's centralized control over care delivery, as currently exercised through the reimbursement system, will be replaced by formularies. The critical task for medical manufacturers will be to get their products and technologies placed on the formularies.
3) The MHLW will introduce quality indicators by using the coefficient of variation already provided for in the current DPC system. The first area of distinction will be JCQHC and/or ISO9001 certification. Other quality indicators will follow. Hospitals that will not or cannot comply with quality indicators will first suffer falling reimbursement rates and then will eventually be driven out of business.
4) Increasingly, expensive medical treatments and technologies receiving regulatory approval will be declared part of the HAMAT system. As a result they will not be reimbursed directly or become part of the DPC formularies.
5) Insurers will start providing supplementary health insurance programs to offer coverage for approved but non-reimbursed medical treatments.

6) Once a critical mass of the population is insured for procedures not covered by the healthcare system, a growing number of hospitals will adopt these technologies and promote this to these patients.
7) There will be two trends among the surviving 'fringe' hospitals, both of them brought about by the decreasing amounts of available reimbursement. Many will become non-acute, long-term care centers. The others will remove themselves completely from government-run programs and target the wealthy and self-insured.

Regardless of what happens – and predictions aside – my greatest hope is that everyone involved in the Japan healthcare debate remains engaged in an honest and productive manner. We need to remember and respect that others often have very different perspectives, and it is my goal that this book helps us understand these diverse viewpoints and the reasons behind them. The answers lie sometime in one perspective and sometimes in another – or combinations thereof – and it is our duty and responsibility to find out which ones are which. A healthy society is one that embraces diversity of perspective and debate. If this book has contributed in any way to either or both of those goals, it has been a success.

Index